THE QUESTION OF QUESTIONS

IS

CHRIST INDEED

THE

SAVIOUR OF THE WORLD?

BY

Rev. THOMAS ALLIN.

SEEING THEN THAT WE HAVE SUCH HOPE, WE USE GREAT PLAINNESS OF SPEECH.
II Cor. iii 12.

LONDON:
T. FISHER UNWIN,
26, PATERNOSTER SQUARE.
1885.

In the interest of creating a more extensive selection of rare historical book reprints, we have chosen to reproduce this title even though it may possibly have occasional imperfections such as missing and blurred pages, missing text, poor pictures, markings, dark backgrounds and other reproduction issues beyond our control. Because this work is culturally important, we have made it available as a part of our commitment to protecting, preserving and promoting the world's literature. Thank you for your understanding.

PREFACE.

No question more momentous than that briefly discussed in the following pages can arise, for the point really at issue is no less than the whole future destiny of our race.

The last quarter of a century has seen a most significant change in the minds of our contemporaries on this question. On every side the old belief in endless torment is passing away; and though it may be enforced on rare occasions in the pulpit, it no longer commands the acceptance of the majority of thoughtful men anywhere.

But while we hail with joy this awakening, we must remember that the void thus left in our Creed requires to be filled up. We have to build as well as to destroy. The old belief in pain without end in Hell has lost its power. What shall take its place? Has the Church no clear and definite message on this all-important point?

The following pages aim at showing that the true answer to this enquiry is to be found in the teaching of Scripture (whose supreme authority we fully recognise), as to the assured and absolute victory of JESUS CHRIST; as to the boundless nature of His empire over all souls. To bring honour to His Cross; to exalt His work of Redemption, as destined one day to restore all things, and thus to reconcile our Creed with the deepest convictions of our moral nature, this is the true meaning of the larger Hope, and not, as so many seem to believe, a desire to make light of sin, to explain away its penalties, or to paint God as a Being weakly tolerant of evil.

In this volume will be, I hope, found a recognition clear and emphatic of the guilt of sin and its assured punishment; nay, it will, I trust, be shewn how, in fact, the larger hope, more fully than any other view, recognises the true evil of sin, and assigns to the Divine penalties their true end.

And so I send forth these pages, claiming for their contents little or no originality, but trusting that in them will be found reasons* clear and Scriptural for this as the true hope of the Gospel, the actual redemption and restoration, not of some men, but of mankind; not of some things, but of all things, through Jesus Christ, our Lord.

---

* I have not presumed to say or to discuss what GOD, in the abstract, can or cannot, will or will not do. The argument here employed is simply this. GOD has both in HIS unwritten revelation of HIMSELF to our moral sense, and in HIS written Word, declared distinctly against the doctrine of endless torment.

CONTENTS.

—:o:—

CHAPTER I.
The Question Stated - - - - - - 1

CHAPTER II.
The Popular Creed Wholly Untenable - - - 17

CHAPTER III.
The Same—(Continued) - - - - - 41

CHAPTER IV.
What The Church Teaches - - - - - 63

CHAPTER V.
What The Old Testament Teaches - - - 85

CHAPTER VI.
What The New Testament Teaches - - - 95

CHAPTER VII.
The Same—(Continued) - - - - - 115

CHAPTER VIII.
The Same—(Continued) - - - - - 141

CHAPTER IX.
The Scriptural Doctrine of the Ages—of Death—
of Judgment—of Fire—of Election - - 165

CHAPTER X.
Summary and Conclusion - - - - - 195

Note—On St. Mark ix., 43-50. 217
  ,,   On the future recovery of the lost,

ERRATUM.

Page 103, line 8—omit "then."

"THE QUESTION STATED."

"Shall not the judge of all the earth do right."—GEN. xviii, 25.

Will the Lord cast off for ever?
And will He be favourable no more?
Hath GOD forgotten to be gracious?
Hath He in anger shut up His tender mercies?
And I said this is my infirmity;
But I will remember the years of the right hand of the Most
High.—PSALM LXXVII, 7-10.

What am I but the creature Thou hast made?
What have I but the blessings Thou hast lent?
What hope I but Thy mercy and Thy love?
I claim the rights of weakness, I the babe
Call on my Sire to shield me from the ills
That still beset my path   *   *   *   *
Thou wilt not hold in scorn the child who dares
Look up to Thee, the Father,   *   *   *

O. W. HOLMES.

CHAPTER I.

THE QUESTION STATED.

1. The following pages are written under the pressure of a deep conviction, that the views generally held, as to the future punishment of the ungodly, wholly fail to satisfy the plain statements of Holy Scripture. The popular creed has maintained itself on a Scriptural basis solely, I believe, by hardening into dogma mere figures of oriental imagery; by mistranslations and misconceptions of the sense of the original (to which our Authorised Version largely contributes): and finally, by completely ignoring a vast body of evidence in favour of the salvation of all men, furnished, as will be shewn, by very numerous passages of the New Testament, no less than by the great principles that pervade the teaching of all Revelation. Again, I write, because persuaded, that however loudly asserted and widely held, the popular belief is at best a Tradition—is not an Article of Faith in the Catholic Church—is taught in no Creed accepted by East and West; nay, is

distinctly opposed to the views of not a few of the holiest and wisest Fathers of the Church, in primitive times ; who, in so teaching, expressed the belief of very many, if not the majority, of Christians in their days.

2. Further, I write, because deeply and painfully convinced of the very serious mischief which has been, and is being produced by the views generally held. They in fact tend, as nothing else ever has, to cause, I had almost said, to justify, the scepticism now so widely spread : they effect this, because they so utterly conflict with any conception we can form of common justice and equity.

3. Therefore, of mercy I shall say little in these pages : it is enough to appeal, when speaking of moral considerations, to that sense of Right and Wrong which is GOD's voice speaking within us. Indeed, among the many misconceptions with which all higher views of the Gospel are assailed, few are more unfounded, than that which asserts, that thus GOD's justice is forgotten in the prominence assigned to HIS mercy. This objection merely shews a complete misapprehension of the views here advocated. For these views do in fact appeal to, and by this appeal recognise, first of all, the justice of GOD. It is precisely the sense of natural equity which GOD has planted within us, that the popular belief in endless torment most deeply wounds.

4. And these considerations are in fact a complete answer to some other objections often heard. " Why disturb men's minds," it is said, "why un- " settle their faith, why not let well alone ? " By all means, I reply, let well alone, but never let ill alone. Men's minds are already disturbed: it is because they are already disturbed, that we would calm them, and would restore the doubters to faith, by pointing them to a larger hope, to a truer Christianity. A graver objection arises, but like the former wholly without foundation in fact. It is said, " By this larger hope you in " fact either weaken or wholly remove all belief in " future punishment. You explain away the guilt " of sin." The very opposite is surely the truth, for you establish future punishment, and with it that sense of the reality of sin (to which conscience testifies) on a firm basis, only when you teach a plan of retribution, which is itself reasonable and credible. A penalty which to our reason and moral sense seems shocking, and monstrous, loses all force as a threat. It has ever been thus in the case of human punishments. And so in the case of Hell. Outwardly believed it has ceased to touch the conscience or greatly to influence the life of Christians. To the mass of men it has become a name and little more (not seldom a jest) ; to the sceptic it has furnished the choicest of his weapons ; to the man of science a mark for loathing and scorn : while, alas, to many a sad and drooping heart, who longs to follow CHRIST more closely, it is the

chief woe and burden of life. But the conscience, when no longer wounded by extravagant dogmas, is most ready to acquiesce in any measure of retribution (how sharp soever it be) which yet does not shock the moral sense, and conflict with its deepest convictions. And so the larger hope most fully recognises at once the guilt of sin, and the need of fitting retribution : nay, it may be claimed for it, that it alone places both on a firm and solid basis, by bringing them into harmony with the verdict of reason, of conscience, and of Holy Scripture.

5. It is better now, for clearness sake, to define that popular view of future punishment, of which I shall often speak. It is briefly this :— That GOD will after death pass on the ungodly a sentence of endless pain, of endless torments ; that from this suffering there is no hope of escape ; that of this torment there is no possible alleviation. That when your imagination has called up a series of ages, in apparently endless succession, all these ages of pain and of agony, undergone by the lost, have diminished their cup of suffering by not so much as one single drop ; their pain is then no nearer ending than before. Those who hold this terrible doctrine to be a part of the "glad tidings of great joy" to men from their Father in Heaven, differ indeed as to the number of the finally lost. some make them to be a majority of mankind, some a minority. Now it may be gravely questioned whether there can be

any doubt at all *from their point of view* on this head. For the texts on which they rely seem, to most minds, if they teach the popular creed at all, to teach, just as clearly, that the lost shall be the majority of men. " Many are called but *few* " are chosen." " Fear not *little* flock." " Narrow " is the way that leadeth to life and *few* there be " that find it." " With *most* of them, GOD was " not well pleased." Indeed, it seems perfectly clear that the popular view requires us to believe in the final loss of the vast majority of our race. For it is only the truly converted in this life (as they assert) who reach Heaven ; and it is beyond all fair question, that of professing Christians only a small portion are truly converted ; to say nothing of the myriads and myriads of those who have died in Paganism. But even waiving this point, the objections to the popular creed are in no way really lightened by our belief, as to the relative numbers of the lost and the saved. The real difficulty consists in the infliction of any such penalty, and not in the number who are doomed to it. Nor need we forget how inconceivably vast must be that number, on the most lenient hypothesis. Take the lowest estimate ; and when you remember the innumerable myriads of our race who have passed away—those now living—and those yet unborn—it becomes clear that the number of the lost must be something in its vastness defying all calculation ; and of these, all, be it remembered, children of the great Parent—all made in HIS image—all redeemed by the life blood of His dear Son; and all shut up for ever and ever (words, of whose awful meaning, no man has, or can have, the very faintest conception) in blackness of darkness, in despair, and in the company of devils.

6. Let me next shew what this Hell of the popular creed really means, so far as human words can dimly convey its horrors, and for this purpose I subjoin the following extracts--one from a Roman Catholic divine, one from Dr. Pusey, and one from Mr. Spurgeon. " Little child, if " you go to Hell there will be a devil at your side " to strike you. He will *go on striking* you every " minute *for ever and ever* without stopping. The " first stroke will make your body as bad as the " body of Job, covered, from head to foot, with " sores and ulcers. The second stroke will make " your body twice as bad as the body of Job. The " third stroke will make your body three times as " bad as the body of Job. The fourth stroke " will make your body four times as bad as the " body of Job. How, then, will your body be, " after the devil has been striking it every moment, " for a hundred million of years without stopp- " ing." Perhaps at this moment, seven o'clock " in the evening, a child is just going into Hell. " To-morrow evening, at seven o'clock, go and " knock at the gates of Hell and ask what the " child is doing. The devils will go and look. " They will come back again and say, *the child is* " *burning*. Go in a week and ask what the child

"is doing; you will get the same answer, *it is
"burning.* Go in a year and ask, the same
"answer comes—*it is burning.* Go in a million
"of years and ask the same question; the answer
"is just the same—*it is burning.* So if you go for
"ever and ever, you will always get the same
"answer *it is burning in the fire.*"—*The Sight of
Hell*, by Rev. J. FURNISS, C.S.S.R., *Permissu
Superiorum*, published by DUFFY, SONS, & Co.
"Gather in one, in your mind, an assembly of all
"those men or women from whom, whether in
"history or in fiction, your memory most shrinks,
"gather in mind all that is most loathsome, most
"revolting * * * conceive the fierce fiery eyes
"of hate, spite, frenzied rage, ever fixed on thee,
"looking thee through and through with hate
"* * * hear those yells of blaspheming, concen-
"trated hate, as they echo along the lurid vault
"of Hell; every one hating every one * * * Yet
"a fixedness in that state in which the hardened
"malignant sinner dies involves, without any
"further retribution of GOD, this endless misery."
—Sermon by Rev. E. B. PUSEY, D.D., Regius
Professor of Hebrew, and Canon of Christ
Church, Oxford (quoted from *Errors and Terrors
of Blind Guides*). "When thou diest thy soul will
"be tormented alone; that will be a Hell for it:
"but at the Day of Judgement thy body will join
"thy soul, and then thou wilt have twin Hells,
"thy soul sweating drops of blood, and thy body
"suffused with agony. In fire, exactly like that
"we have on earth, thy body will lie, asbestos like,

"for ever unconsumed, all thy veins roads for the "feet of pain to travel on, every nerve a string, "on which the Devil shall for ever play his "diabolical tune of Hell's unutterable lament."— Sermon on the *Resurrection of the Dead*, by Rev. C. H. SPURGEON (Cited by Archdeacon FARRAR in *Mercy and Judgement*.) Awful as are these quotations, I must repeat, that they give no adequate idea at all of the horrors of Hell; for that which is the very sting of its terrors—their unendingness—is beyond our power really to conceive, even approximately: so totally incommensurable are the ideas of time and of eternity.

7. But it will be said, we no longer believe in a material Hell—no longer teach a lake of real fire. I might well ask, on your theory of interpreting Scripture, what right have you so to teach? But let me rather welcome this change of creed, so far as it is a sign of an awakening moral sense. Yet, your plea, in mitigation of the horror your doctrines inspire, cannot be admitted; for when you offer for acceptance a spiritual, rather than a material flame, who is there that cannot see that the real difficulty is the same, whether you suppose man's body burned or his spirit tortured? It may be even maintained, fairly, that a Hell which torments the higher part, is rather an aggravated than a mitigated penalty.

8. Merely to state this doctrine, in any form, is to refute it for very many minds. So deeply

does it wound, what is best and holiest in us;
indeed, as I shall try to shew further on, it is, for
all practical purposes, found incredible, even by
those who honestly profess to believe it. This
terrible difficulty, felt and acknowledged in all
ages, has been largely met for the Roman
Catholic, by the doctrine of Purgatory, which
became developed as the belief in endless torment,
gradually supplanted that earlier and better faith,
which *alone* finds expression in the two really
Catholic and Ancient Creeds, faith in *Everlasting
Life*. How immense must have been the relief
thus afforded, is evident, when we remember that
the least sorrow, however imperfect, the very
slightest desire for reconciliation with GOD, though
deferred to the last moment of existence, was
believed to free the dying sinner from the pains
of Hell, no matter how aggravated his sins may
have been. Among the Reformed Communions
this difficulty was met, no doubt, by a silent
incredulity—often unconscious—yet ever increasing, on the part of the great majority;
indeed, some divines have at all times, both in
England and on the Continent, openly avowed
their disbelief in endless torments. This growing
incredulity has found, in our day, open expression, in a remarkable theory, that of Conditional
Immortality (itself a revival of an earlier belief).
This doctrine, briefly stated, teaches, that man is
naturally mortal, that only in JESUS CHRIST is
immortality conferred on the righteous—that
the ungodly shall be judged, and after due

punishment, annihilated.

9. Of this dogma I shall at once say, that, while it degrades man, it fails to vindicate GOD. A writer, whose words I am glad to adopt, speaks of it as " that most wretched and cowardly of all " theories, which supposes the soul to be natur- " ally mortal, and that GOD will resuscitate the " wicked to torment them for a time and then " finally extinguish them. I can see no ground " for this view in Scripture but in mistaken inter- " pretations, and it does not meet the real difficulty " at all, for it supposes that evil has in such cases " finally triumphed, and that GOD had no resource " but to punish and extinguish it : which is essen- " tially the very difficulty felt by the sceptical " mind. I have called it cowardly, for it surren- " ders the true nobility of man, his natural " immortality, in a panic—at an objection, and " like all cowardice, fails in securing safety."— *Donellan Lectures*, p. 31, by Rev. Dr. QUARRY. Besides, this theory has evidently the characters of a makeshift, an after thought, The conscience has been shocked by the popular creed, and has taken refuge in the first shelter that offered. Men have seen death and destruction repeatedly denounced in the Bible as the sinner's doom, and they conclude, contrary to the whole spirit of Holy Scripture, that death, in its pages, implies annihilation But this view is, in the case of the Old Testament, quite unfounded ; for earthly destruction is all that the expressions, there relied

on, really teach ; and in the case of the New
Testament is completely inadequate : because,
there, death and destruction have a far wider
significance, and one far deeper. Nay, as I hope
to point out, there is in New Testament usage
a deep spiritual connection between death and
life ; death becomes the path to, and the condition
of life.

10. Another view adopted by a number, probably extremely large, and increasing, differs altogether from that last stated. Those who hold it
have had their eyes opened to the fact, that the
New Testament contains very many long neglected
texts which teach the salvation of all men. They
have also learned enough to have their faith
gravely shaken in the popular interpretation of
the texts usually quoted in proof of endless pain.
The theory of conditional immortality fails to
satisfy such men. They see that it is altogether
unsuccessful in meeting the real difficulty of the
popular creed, *i.e.*, the triumph of evil over good,
of Satan over the Saviour of man, and therefore
over GOD. They perceive, too, the narrow and
arbitrary basis on which it rests in appealing to
Holy Scripture. And so they decline to entertain it as any solution of the question, and say,
" We are not able to accept any theory definitely
" of the future of man, because we do not see that
" anything has been clearly revealed. Enough has
" been disclosed to shew to us that GOD is love,
" and we are content to believe, that happen what

"will, all will ultimately be shewn to be the "result of love divine."

11. It is impossible to avoid sympathy with much of this view; but does it meet the needs of the case—is it adequate to the wants of the human heart—does it satisfy the conscience—does it give fair and full weight to the glorious promises of the Gospel, long hidden but now coming to light? I am persuaded that it does not; I am also persuaded that its very vagueness is fatal to any general acceptance of this teaching; we have a right to enquire, and to know, not indeed the details of our future life, but this broad fact, is there hope for our race—shall we indeed reach a haven of rest? Involuntary passengers, in this solemn voyage between life and death, we cannot rest without knowing some thing more definite of our destination: and we believe that we have in the Bible some definite hope, some clear and distinct information. Life and immortality, we are assured, have been brought to light by JESUS CHRIST. HE has assured us that HIS will is to save all men, and we cannot imagine HIS will not being effectual. HE promises, not by one or two but by all HIS holy Prophets, a time of restitution of all things, not some things. HE tells us how the leaven of the kingdom shall leaven the whole lump; how the Good Shepherd shall seek on and on till he find the stray sheep. HE assures us that, if in ADAM all die, in CHRIST shall all be made alive. HE points to the certain

victory, when every enemy overcome, and the glorious end reached, GOD shall be ALL in ALL. With these, and many other so explicit promises on every hand; men will not, cannot, ought not, to be content to believe that nothing definite is to be gathered, as to the destiny of our race, from Holy Scripture.

12. In opposition to both these theories stand the views here advocated, which have been always held by some in the Catholic Church, nay, which represent, I believe, most nearly its primitive teaching. These views are, I know, now widely held by the learned, the devout, and the thoughtful in our own and in other Communions. Briefly stated, they amount to this:—That we have ample warrant, alike from reason—from the observed facts and analogies of human life—from our best and truest moral instincts—and from Holy Scripture itself, to entertain a firm hope that GOD our Father's design and purpose is, and has ever been, to save every child of ADAM's race.

"THE
"POPULAR CREED WHOLLY UNTENABLE."

"These questions * * * educated men and women of all "classes and denominations, orthodox, be it remembered, as well as "unorthodox, are asking and will ask more and more till they receive "an answer. And if we of the clergy cannot give them an answer, "which accords with their conscience and reason * * * then "evil times will come, both for the clergy and the Christian religion, "for many a year henceforth."—Canon KINGSLEY—*Water of Life*, p. 71.

"The answer which the popular theology has been tendering for "centuries past will not be accepted much longer * * * I "disclaim any desire to uphold that theology which I have never "aided in propagating."—Rev. Dr. LITTLEDALE—*Contemporary Review, 1878.*

"Man is based on Hope, he has properly no other possession but "Hope; this habitation of his is named the place of Hope."— CARLYLE—*French Revolution*, p. 35.

"One's heart rejoices at the awakening that is coming upon the "rising generation."—*Letters from a Mystic*, p. 25.

CHAPTER II.

"THE POPULAR CREED WHOLLY UNTENABLE."

The next step will be to state, more in detail, the various considerations that render it impossible to accept the popular view of future punishment. My first appeal shall be to that primary revelation of Himself, which GOD has implanted in the heart and conscience of man. I am merely expressing the deepest and most mature, though often unspoken, conviction of millions of earnest Christian men and women, when I assert, that to reconcile the popular creed, or any similar belief in Hell, with the most elementary ideas of justice, equity, and goodness (not even to mention mercy), is wholly and absolutely impossible. Thus this belief destroys the *only ground* on which it is possible to erect any religion at all, for it sets aside the primary convictions of the moral sense; and thus paralyses that, by which alone we are capable of religion.* If GOD be not good, just,

---

* Those who object to this position are invited to state clearly on what other basis they propose to erect the fabric of religion in the heart and conscience of man. I am capable of religion, solely, because within me GOD has placed a moral sense: therefore, to destroy this is, with it, to destroy all religion.

and true, in *the human acceptation of these terms*, then the whole basis of revelation vanishes. For let me once more repeat that, if God be not good in our human sense of the word, I have no guarantee that He is true in our sense of truth. If what is called goodness in God in the Bible, should prove to be that which we call badness in man, then how can I be assured that, what is called truth in God, may not really be that which in man is called falsehood? Thus no valid communication—no revelation—from God to man is possible; for no reliance can, on this view, be placed on His veracity.

The popular view to you is familiar, and perhaps you do not realise its true bearing, or the light in which it really presents the *character* of God. But consider how this dogma of endless torture must strike an enquirer after God, one outside the pale of Christianity, but sincerely desirous of learning the truth. There are such men—there are many such. You tell this enquirer that God is not Almighty only, but all Good; that God is indeed Love; that God is his Father. But these terms are words *without any meaning at all*, if they have not their common ordinary sense when applied to God. Such a man will say, you tell me God is good, but what *acts* are these you assign to Him? He is a Father; but He brings into being myriads of hapless creatures, knowing that there is in store for them a doom unutterably awful. He calls into existence these creatures, whether they will or no ; though the bottomless pit is yawning to receive them, and the flames ready to devour them. The question is not, whether they might have escaped ; the real question is, *do they in fact escape*, and *does He know* that they will not escape. And you assure me that this Great Being is Almighty ! is Love essential ! is the Parent of every one of these creatures, who are doomed and damned ! What *fair* answer do you propose to give to these questions if addressed to you ?

But probably the way in which most people satisfy their own minds, when doubts arise, as to the endless nature of future torment is this. " Endless pain and torment is but the result of " sin freely chosen, and finally persisted in by " the sinner," it is said. Now, let us look more closely at this statement, and see what it really means. Doubtless all will admit that God is Almighty ; that God is all true ; that God is all good ; that He is, in short, infinite in power, in truth, and in goodness. But when you tell me, that it is possible for the human will to resist the divine, you are, in fact, denying each of these divine attributes. You deny that God is Almighty, for you make man's will stronger than His. You deny God's veracity, for He has over and over asserted, that to Him every knee shall bow, and every tongue confess. You deny God's infinite goodness, for the obstinate and final choice of evil, by any of His creatures, is a triumph of evil over good.

And further still, though I do not profess here to discuss the various questions involved in man's free will, yet there is something that ought to be said, as to the extent of free choice, which man really has—something not to be lost sight of in deciding this question of free choice. In the first place, man can exercise no choice at all, as to the strength of that will he receives; no choice at all, as to the circumstances that surround him, in infancy and childhood, and which colour his whole life; no choice at all as to the original weakness of his nature, and its inherent tendency to evil. More, still, he can exercise no choice at all, on this *vital* question, whether he will or will not have laid on him the awful perils, in which, on the popular view, the mere fact of life involves him. You tell me of the terrible risks of human life, of its infinite responsibilities; you are fond of enlarging on the taint of original sin, on our inability to help ourselves. True, but what does all this prove? surely this, that a good Being would not have bestowed such a gift, except with a purpose, clear and definite, that all should issue in good. "Nothing," says Bishop NEWTON, " is more con- " trariant to the divine nature and attributes, " than for GOD to bestow existence on any " being, whose destiny HE fore-knows must " terminate in wretchedness without recovery." —*Dissert. on the Final State of Man.* " With "great reverence I venture to express the "conviction, that if the great Being fore-knew "that eternal misery—conscious suffering— "would be the doom, of even a single creature, "it is incredible that HE would have given exis- "tence to that creature."—*Creator and Creation*, Dr. J. YOUNG. Yes it is incredible! and this is, alas, but one of many incredible things the popular creed is trying to make men accept.

Yes, the question is essentially this, and no argument can evade this enquiry :—Is GOD good, and is HE a just GOD, as men use these terms, or is he not? Indeed if the GOD we worship be not good, as we call goodness, it were better for us not to worship him at all : better for us to worship nothing at all, than to worship an evil Deity. But the popular view represents GOD as doing that which the most degraded human being would not do. " This view," says the Rev. Dr. LITTLEDALE, "puts GOD on a "moral level with the devisers of the most "savagely malignant revenge known to history." *Contemporary Review*, 1878.

Again, a difficulty equally grave, is the following :—That the popular view, while admitting GOD's power and goodness to be infinite, yet teaches that evil shall ultimately prevail—a position obviously untenable, and indeed absurd. " Order and right *cannot but prevail* finally, in a "universe under HIS Government."—BUTLER'S

Analogy (Introduction). For argue as you please, refine, explain away, it continues still an *insuperable* difficulty, on the popular view, or any mere modification of it, that the DEVIL is victor and triumphs over GOD and goodness. It is nothing at all to the purpose to allege, either that those who perish finally have chosen evil of their own will, or that all evil beings are shut up in chains and torment : it is the very permanence of evil in any shape : its continued presence —*no matter from what cause*—that constitutes the triumph of the Evil One.

Again, so revolting to our moral nature is the popular creed, that it, more than any other cause, as has been said, produces the most widespread unbelief. "Compared with this," remarks J. S. MILL, "all other objections to Christianity "sink into insignificance." Let me speak plainly. Too long—far too long—have the clergy been silent; content to complain of a scepticism, of which a doctrine they continue to teach (without, I believe in many cases, more than a languid and traditional acceptance of it) is a main cause. For my part it seems far nearer the truth to complain of, to be amazed at the extent of human credulity. What folly is there that men have not been in all ages only too willing to believe—what false prophet has ever wanted followers—what craze has ever lacked disciples ? Nay, in this England of ours, of whose scepticism you complain, here too what limit can you assign to human credulity? Take the great Anglo-Israel craze, the Spirit-rapping mania, the Tichborne Claimant craze, take a thousand others: the public is ready for one and all; and yet you speak of unbelief as rampant! If it be rampant, be very sure that you must have greviously overstrained the faculty of belief, by doctrines impossible for man to believe. Nay, worse still, by teaching these evil traditions (for they are no more) as part of the revelation of that GOD whose blessed SON tasted death for every man. Yes, the peculiar horror of the popular creed is, that it sets up evil as an object of worship—of reverence—of love.

Now if the Gospel of our LORD JESUS CHRIST be any one thing, more than another, it is good news; and not this merely, but good news to all men; not to the elect, or to the good, but to every son of our common parent ADAM. It means that we all have reason to bless GOD for our creation—as the Church teaches us to pray—not surely that we may have reason, but that we have reason, a very different thing. What but this is the meaning of that touching verse, in which our LORD, *by a hint*, as HIS manner is so often in conveying the deepest truth, imparts —to those who have ears to hear—so much, when HE says:—" A woman when she is in " travail hath sorrow, because her hour has " come; but as soon as she is delivered of the " child she forgetteth her anguish for *joy that a* "*man is born into the world?*" I ask then, have you, who complain of scepticism, made certain that *your own teaching* is not, in great part, the very cause of this evil? Are you certain that you are preaching not merely a possible salvation, followed by a probable Hell, but an actual deliverance wrought out for each man by the Saviour? Do you yourself believe, in the plain natural sense of the words, that, " HE hath been " manifested to put away sin by the sacrifice of " HIMSELF ; the original imports an actual des- " truction of sin?"—*Heb.* ix, 26. Have you ever taught this as good news, that HE came, "that through death HE might destroy him that "had the power of death, *i.e.*, the Devil?"—*Heb.* ii, 14.

Yes, the question of all questions is, Is GOD indeed love, is the Gospel really good news, not possible but *actual*, real glad · tidings? All around us, thoughtful men are more than ever reflecting on these points ; what answer do you propose to give? They are thus enquiring— pondering—of themselves, of their lot, of their hopes and fears in the future :—I find myself in this world (so run their thoughts) ; on me are laid, *whether I will or no*, the awful responsibilities of time, and of eternity At my entrance on life I received not a nature upright, but one already fallen, and that for no fault of mine ; stained, and that with no sin of mine. And to this nature so weak, so fallen, so helpless, come, in every variety, temptations, wiles, and allurements such that no man has wholly withstood, or can withstand, their subtle power. Now if this be a part of my probation, if it be a path to better things, I can in submission—nay, in gladness even—bend to my Creator's will: I can take courage, and, though faint, still pursue the narrow path that leads to life. But how can I believe that, a loving Creator—all powerful as He is all good—does so arrange, does so permit, that, for any one soul, this sad and fallen estate of human nature shall prove but the portal to endless woe. So men reason. I do not wonder, I rejoice, that they have ceased to believe, that a divine parent can do that, which an earthly parent could not do without eternal infamy. For next imagine any degree of folly and sin, that can stain human nature, to be accumulated on the head of some one sinful child of man, and I ask, can you believe that any human father, any mother, that once loved that child, could bring herself calmly to sentence her offspring to an endless Hell; nay, herself to keep that child there in anguish that never shall terminate.

But further, there is this most grave difficulty: all sin, be it never so black (and God forbid that I should even seem to weaken its blackness), is but finite. Yet, for these finite sins, you tell me an infinite punishment is the due penalty. But finite and infinite are wholly incommensurable terms. Have you ever set yourself seriously to realise what punishment, protracted *for ever and ever* indeed means? In fact, the idea of illimitable time mocks our utmost efforts to grasp it. "The imagination can come to a stand "nowhere or ever. On the mind goes, heaping "up its millions and billions and quadrillions of "millions. It is to no purpose, time without a "beginning—without an end—still confronts it. "As thus thought of, the mind recoils from the "contemplation, horrified, paralysed with terror. "O, what say ye to this, ye orthodox defenders "of the dogma of everlasting punishment—*your-* "*selves safe* in the everlasting arms."—*Good the Final Goal of Ill*, p. 113. Yes, it is the innate sense of justice and equity that is utterly outraged by the popular doctrine. Would it not be better to set these things straight before you complain of the wide-spread prevalence of scepticism?

Further, it is said—for what have not men said, at what straw have they not grasped, in vain attempts to support a doctrine that each day crumbles under their touch? It has actually been argued that a sin is infinite, because committed against an infinite being: so that, I suppose, to rob a nobleman would be a greater crime, morally, than to deprive a beggar of his last penny!

Again it is said, that perhaps the flames of Hell may be needed to terrorize some far distant sinful orb; that rebels against GOD, in some other planet, may read, by the light of Hell-fire, the dangers of sin. Yes, it has been gravely alleged that a Being, whose name is Love, will light, and keep alight through unending ages, a ghastly living torch for such a purpose as this— a torch—each atom of which is composed of a lost soul, once His child, once made in His image, once redeemed by the Cross of His dear Son! You know this has been taught, and yet you actually complain that men are sceptical, and that thoughtful artisans reject such a creed with scorn.

And let us not forget how much this belief has fostered in man a spirit of cruelty. It is sad, but true, to recollect how much of the suffering inflicted by man, on his brother man, has been due, directly or indirectly, to the belief in Hell. How many ghastly fires has it not helped to light up here on earth, each containing a living, agonizing human being, often thus punished for a trifling error in creed? For if men believed that GOD would light up the gloomy fires of Hell, and keep them blazing to all eternity, it was an easy and a natural step, to set up in His name a little copy of His justice, and thus, as it were, to anticipate GOD's sentence. "As the souls of "heretics are hereafter to be eternally burning in "Hell," such was the reasoning of Queen MARY in defence of her awful persecution, "there can "be nothing more proper than for me to imitate "the divine vengeance, by burning them here on "earth." I say, that however familiar this may be, it is necessary to ponder well the sad facts, for by awaking a righteous horror and indignation we may often most effectually combat such dogmas. And more must be said, not alone have the popular doctrines done all this, but they have greatly influenced for evil the general course of human legislation, and human thought. You may assuredly find traces of the baneful influence of a belief in Hell-fire, in a spirit of cruelty infused into many laws once current, now, and justly, abhorred by all. Nay, it has indeed poisoned the very fount of pity and love by representing Him, whose we are, and before whom we bow, as calmly looking on during the endless cycles of eternity at the agony of myriads upon myriads of His creatures.

But further, it must be added, that by this shocking creed the moral tone is lowered all round, wherever it is accepted. Men are by it familiarized with the idea of suffering and sin as permanent facts. They have even in some sort learned to consider Heaven as dependant upon the belief in an eternal Hell. Nay, I will say, that even the holiest men believing the popular creed are unconsciously depraved, morally and spiritually. You will find for instance, one so holy and so revered as Keble, pleading (see Hymn for second Sunday in Lent) for endless torment, on the plea that if this were not true, then endless bliss in Heaven would also not be true. To put it plainly, he would, as I understand his words, purchase Heaven's unending bliss at the terrible cost of the endless, hopeless torture of the lost! Here I will only say, that I know not whether his logic, or his moral tone be more unsound. Do but for the moment compare the spirit of KEBLE with, I will not say the spirit of CHRIST, but with that of ST. PAUL, who wished himself accursed from CHRIST if thereby he could save his brethren! As to KEBLE's argument, that will be fully answered in considering, in a later chapter, *St. Matthew* xxv, 46. Meantime, as a further illustration, I copy the following from a Periodical lying before me :—" I " was talking the other day with a very learned " Catholic ecclesiastic, who told me that he had " been called on to give the last Sacraments to a " poor Irishman. He found his penitent with " some free-thinking friend, who was arguing " that there was no Hell. The dying Celt raised " himself up with much indignation ; 'no Hell,' " he exclaimed, ' then where is the poor man's " *consolation* ? ' "

And this difficulty goes further still : for we cannot suppose that the saints in Heaven are without the memory of the past. Even DIVES, in the flames of Hades, remembers with pity his brethren. But unless you make the impossible supposition, that the blessed lose all memory in Heaven, then they must either suffer *keenly* at the thoughts of the torments of their dear ones lost in Hell, and tormented for ever and ever; or they must be on a *lower level*, morally and spiritually, than was even DIVES, choose which alternative you please.

You may not perhaps know the sad lengths to which theologians have gone (the moral tone, as I have said before, having been depraved by their awful creed), and I therefore subjoin a few extracts—for which I am indebted to Canon FARRAR. They are from sources so widely apart as a medieval schoolman, and a modern Puritan. "That the saints may *enjoy* their beatitude more "thoroughly, and give more abundant thanks for "it to GOD, *a perfect sight* of the punishment of "the damned is granted them."—*St. Thomas—Summa* iii, *Suppl. Qu.* xciii, 1. Take another instance, from PETER LOMBARD, "Therefore the "elect shall go forth to see the torments of the "impious, seeing which they will not be grieved, "but will be *satiated with joy* at the sight of the "*unutterable* calamity of the impious."—*Senten.* iv, 50. Again hear another from a modern divine, "The *view of the misery of the damned* "will *double* the ardour of the love and gratitude "of the saints in Heaven." This is the opinion of the once famous JONATHAN EDWARDS. Another American divine uses even stronger language. "This display of the divine character," said S. HOPKINS, "will be most *entertaining* to all who "love GOD—will give them the *highest* and *most* "*ineffable pleasure. Should the fire of this eternal*

"*punishment cease, it would in a great measure
"obscure the light of Heaven, and put an end to
"a great part of the happiness and glory of the
"blessed.*"—*Works*, vol. iv, *Serm*. xiii. To this
the belief in Hell-fire has reduced the ministers
of CHRIST, to penning passages like the above
(easily to be multiplied)—passages, than which
all literature does not contain anything more
revolting. I must ask you, as a relief from these
truly fearful words, to read the following touching picture (not this time from an ecclesiastical
source):—

> What if a soul redeemed, a spirit that loved
> While yet on earth, and was beloved in turn,
> And still remembered every look and tone
> Of that dear earthly sister, who was left
> Among the unwise virgins at the gate:
> Itself admitted with the bridegroom's train,—
> What if this spirit redeemed, amid the host
> Of chanting angels, in some transient lull
> Of the eternal anthem, heard the cry
> Of its lost darling, whom in evil hour
> Some wilder pulse of nature led astray,
> And left an outcast in a world of fire,
> Condemned to be the sport of cruel fiends,
> Sleepless, unpitying, masters of the skill
> To wring the maddest ecstasies of pain
> From worn-out souls that only ask to die,—
> *Would it not long to leave the bliss of Heaven,*
> *Bearing a little water in its hand*
> *To moisten those poor lips that plead in vain*
> *With Him we call our Father?*
> O. W. HOLMES.—*The Poet at the Breakfast Table.*

Nor have I yet done with this point. I say
next that the popular creed does *in fact* teach

men to think lightly of sin. This seems a paradox, and no doubt you wonder: but consider for a moment what the fact is. Tell me, that GOD will permit an eternal Hell, with its miserable population of the lost, to go on sinning to all eternity; and what idea is it you really convey to me? It is, I reply, *toleration of sin*. *Have you ever thought of this?* I avail myself of the words of a thoughtful writer, and say, " that nothing so " effectually teaches men to bear with sin as the " popular creed, because we profess to believe that " GOD will bear with it for ever."--*Letters from a Mystic.* On the other hand it is, I believe, often precisely those who most deeply feel the taint and evil of sin who reject most completely the popular creed; for in proportion to their horror at sin, is the depth of their conviction, that sin cannot go on for ever. There is also a very serious question—to which I venture to allude in passing —if sin is to endure for ever in Hell, must it not increase and go on increasing through all eternity. Think to what point of horror the accumulated sin of the myriads of the lost will have reached, when even a few of the cycles of eternity are over: and this vast and inconceivable horror and taint is to go *on*, and *on*, and *on*, for *ever*, and *ever*, and *ever increasing*, under the rule of HIM who is of purer eyes than to behold iniquity!

There is again, a difficulty—an impossibility rather—in reconciling the popular creed with the view, which either Holy Scripture or reason give of punishment—its object and nature. Apart from all question of its justice—apart, too, from the horror it excites—endless, hopeless torment, is a useless, and therefore a wanton, infliction: it is a mere barbarity, because it is only vindictive, and in no sense remedial. Punishment is, on any true theory, no less remedial than vindictive, nay, is essentially remedial and corrective. Our day has seen a complete revolution in the ideas men form of punishment and its end: in few things has the advance been more marked over the past, than in our recognition of the true object of penalty. Not that mere pain is looked on as necessarily remedial, but with the penalty, we now seek to combine corrective influences; the whole spirit of punishment has been altered with the change in men's minds, and a higher tone now every where prevails. But let me ask, *to whom* is due this marked change for the better, in our ideas of punishment? Surely to that Great Being who guides and orders by HIS providence all human things! This being so, it is wholly incredible to assign to the divine punishments, this very character of mere vindictiveness, which men have in all enlightened systems abandoned. This is, I repeat, impossible to believe, for when GOD chastises it is *for our profit*, as the Bible says. HE punishes, as an old Father puts it, *medicinally.* Yes, it is impossible to believe the ordinary dogma, for if GOD does indeed by HIS providence—by HIS Spirit—direct and enlighten men's minds, leading them to higher and truer thoughts on this subject (as on all others), then to suppose that HIS own punishments are regulated on the very system, which HE has taught us to abandon, is truly impossible.

Nor can I close this subject without remarking that there is a highly significant expression found in that very passage, most often on the lips of the defenders of endless pain, which yet, curiously enough, furnishes the material for an answer to their creed: I speak of *St. Matthew* xxv, 46. The term there applied to the punishment of the ungodly is not the ordinary Greek word to denote penalty, but it is a term (*Kolasis*) denoting, literally, *pruning*, *i.e.*, a corrective chastisement — an age-long (but reformatory) punishment. Surely the choice of this particular word, to designate the future suffering of the ungodly, is full of significance : unless, indeed, any one should prefer to think that *chance* dictated its selection in this inspired sentence. But should you hear it brought as an argument against the larger hope, that its advocates deny the retributive character of punishment: assuredly this is not so. They merely assert, that while punishment is truly retributive, its paramount end is not this, but the higher aim of amending by chastisement. (See on this whole subject the remarks on GOD's judgements in a subsequent chapter.)

I must also remind you of another feature of the popular belief, which seems to present a great difficulty; it is what I must call its paltriness, its poorness. Let us for the moment, not think of GOD as a good, loving, and righteous Being. Let us now simply regard HIM as great, as irresistible, as almighty. Viewed thus, how difficult is it to accept that account which the ordinary creed gives us of this Being's attempt at the rescue of HIS fallen creature man. An Almighty Being puts forth every effort to gain a certain end; sends inspired men to teach others; works miracles, signs, wonders in Heaven and on earth, all for this end of man's safety; nay, at the last, sends forth HIS own SON—very GOD—HIMSELF Almighty. The Almighty SON stoops not alone to take our nature on HIM, but lower still—far lower—stoops to degradation; meekly accepts insult and scourging, bends to the bitter Cross even, and all this to gain a certain end. And yet, they tell us, this end is not gained after all. man is not saved, for countless myriads are in fact left to hopeless, endless misery; and that though for *every one of these lost ones*, so to speak, has been shed the life blood of GOD's own SON. Now, if I may be permitted to speak freely, it is wholly inconceivable that the definite plan of an Almighty Being should end in failure—that this should be the result of the agony of the eternal SON.

And continue this thought. If we think of

God at all worthily, we cannot help thinking of Him as working for high and worthy ends. Therefore we cannot help thinking of Him, as in creation, working for some end worthy of Himself. But what end does the popular creed assign to Him? A creation broken, marred, mutilated, ruined, and so to continue for ever. A creation ending in misery, pain, woe unutterable, to infinite numbers of the created: and all this misery and horror brought into sharper relief by a vain and fruitless attempt to save all: by a purpose of love declared *to all*, and yet *not* in fact reaching all: a creation which is the portal for one half, or more of the created to Hell! And you gravely ask thoughtful enquirers, to believe this; to believe that for such an end, and contemplating these horrors destined never to cease, the morning stars are described as singing together, and all the sons of God *shouting for joy* on the morning of creation.

But again, there comes this very serious obstacle to accepting the popular creed. I shall state it thus, either this creed is true or false. If false—the question is ended. If true—can you explain to me this strange fact, that *nobody acts as if he believed it?* I say this, for any man who so believed, and who possessed but a spark of common humanity—to say nothing of charity—could not rest, day or night, so long as one sinner remained who might be saved. To this all would give place: pleasure, learning, business, art, literature ; nay, life itself would be too short for the terrible warnings, the burning entreaties, the earnest pleadings, that would be needed to rouse sinners from their apathy, and to pluck them from endless tortures. Ask me what you will, but do not ask me to believe that any human being, who is convinced that perhaps his own child, his wife, his friend, his neighbour even, is in danger of endless torment, could, if *really* persuaded of this, live as men now live, even the best men. Who can avoid the inevitable conclusion that its warmest adherents really, though unconsciously, find their dogmas absolutely incredible? " The world would be *one vast mad-* "*house*," says the American scholar HALLSTED, " if a realising and continued pressure of such a " doctrine was present." Remark again how this doctrine breaks down the moment it is really put to the test. Take a common case : a man dies—active, benevolent, useful in life, but not a religious man, not devout. By the popular creed, such a man has gone to Hell for ever. But who really believes that ? nay, instinctively, our words grow softer when we speak of the dead, in all cases.

" THE
" POPULAR CREED WHOLLY UNTENABLE."

"Far be it from us to make light of the demerit of sin. But endless punishment—I admit my inability (I would say it reverently) to admit this belief together with a belief in the Divine goodness—the belief that GOD is Love, that HIS tender mercies are over all HIS works."—JOHN FOSTER, on *Future Punishment.*

"Can these dark dogmas be true of a Father who bids us be perfect as HE is, in that HE sends HIS sun to shine on the evil and the good, and the rain on the just and the unjust. Or of a SON who so loved the world that HE died to save the world—and surely not in vain."—C. KINGSLEY.

"And now that we are emerging from the shadow of the doctrine, we look with a shudder and ask ourselves, how it was possible that Christian men should believe it, and should connect such unutterable horrors with the administration of a Being, who has given to us in Calvary the measure of HIS love."—Rev. J. BALDWIN BROWN—*Cont. Review.*

CHAPTER III.

"THE POPULAR CREED WHOLLY UNTENABLE.'

Pursuing our argument—let me next point out a practical difficulty of the gravest kind which arises on the popular view. It is this: how can you on any such principle deal fairly or equitably with the mass of men? Let us speak plainly: do tell me who and what are the great, nay, the *overwhelming* majority of the baptized? They are assuredly neither wholly bad, nor wholly good; they are neither bad enough for Hell, nor good enough for Heaven. Now how can you adapt your theory to this state of things, which is, I think, quite impossible to deny? Look around you, survey the mass of mankind: of how few, how very few can you affirm that they are truly devout, converted, holy, Christ-like; take which term you please. Can you affirm this of one in ten; in twenty; in a hundred even, of those baptized into JESUS CHRIST? Take as an illustration any English parish you please. Take its entire population, what are they, how many are the really good? Take any village, or select some one of our English towns, muster its whole population in imagination, how many true, holy servants of JESUS CHRIST will you find there? The mass, what are they? Do meet this question, and look the facts straight in the face. What is to be the doom of the mass of baptized Christians—they are not holy, but are they bad? Nobody out of the pulpit—and seldom there in these days—ventures to assert any such thing. Indeed there is abundant good in this crowd of human beings, and still more, there is almost infinite capacity for goodness, amid the evil. Everywhere you will find unselfish parents, hard workers, loving sisters, true friends; everywhere traces, distinct enough amid all the sin, yes, and traces in abundance of goodness, kindness, patience, self-sacrifice, sometimes carried even to great lengths. Let an emergency arise, let sickness come, what devotion does it not call forth—what love unstinted, what self-forgetfulness? Now your system, that which you call the good news brought from Heaven by JESUS CHRIST, forces you to believe that GOD will consign all these hapless children of HIS, because unconverted, unrenewed, to a doom which in its lightest form is awful beyond all powers of imagination; to the company of devils for ever and ever; to darkness unbroken by a single ray of light. Permit me one question more, would not any creed, *anything*, be a positive relief from such *a gospel* as this of yours? Can there be a mockery more solemn, more emphatic, than to call this any part of the glad tidings of great joy? Is it not time for the clergy, not merely in private to ponder these things, convinced or half-convinced of their truth, but to speak out as in GOD's name—as GOD's ministers?

And while I am speaking of men as they are, and of the life they lead, let me add here a statement of another very grave difficulty in the way of accepting an endless Hell as the doom of any man, the issue of any life. Wherever human beings exist, in what form of community it matters not, in what climate or under what conditions of life soever, there is found *everywhere* a deep spontaneous belief, call it feeling, instinct, what you please, that connects the marriage tie and the birthday with joyful associations, with mirth and gladness. Now why is this—has it no meaning? So deep an instinct, one so truly natural and spontaneous as this comes surely from the CREATOR of all. HIS voice it is that bids the Bridegroom rejoice over the Bride, that bids the heart of the mother overflow with tenderness towards her babe. This being so, again let me put the question, and ask, *why* has this been so ordered? It is GOD who has so ordered; do you think HE has had no purpose in so doing, no message to convey to those who have ears to hear? Is it possible that our Heavenly Father should bid HIS creatures everywhere to rejoice with a special joy at the marriage feast, at the natal hour, if these births were in fact destined to add largely to the ranks of Hell, to the hosts of evil? Do think over the matter calmly, and ask yourself if that is possible, if you can believe any such thing.

And as you think it over, take with you these words of JESUS CHRIST (that hint so much), need I once more quote them? They remind us how the mother, in the " perilous birth " hath sorrow; but add, that all that sorrow is swallowed up in joy, "*joy* that a man is born into the " world." Dwell on these words that you may grasp all they convey. Indeed in this lies the whole matter. It is *a joy* that a man—any man—should be born into the world. See how wide the words are! If you tell me it is but a blind instinct of the mother, yes, I reply, it is this very blindness, as you call it, of the instinct that constitutes its force, for it thus betrays its origin; it is implanted; and by whom? by the Great Parent, for it is spontaneous and betrays HIS hand. Do you ask me to believe that HE has done this without a meaning, without a certain purpose of good? Can I believe that our Father bids any mother's heart to stir with joy at the sight of her infant while HE knows that this infant is destined to be, will be, one day shut up into endless torment?

And again, can you reconcile your theory of endless torment awaiting so large a portion of our

race with that natural thirst for joy, that longing for happiness each one finds within. It matters not whether this has been slowly developed, or created at one stroke, all that matters to this argument is its *naturalness*, its *universality*. This longing for happiness cannot then have been accidental, there must be in it a design on the Creator's part. Now, do say, what that design can have been? To mock us—to mock any one of us—is that possible? " If the popular theory
" of future endless torment were true, what
" sublime mockery would there be in placing poor
" wretches first upon earth, where are heard the
" merry shouts of careless children, the joyous
" song of birds, where above our heads,

 'With constant kindly smile the sleepless stars,
 'Keep everlasting watch * * * '

" where beneath our feet the delicate beauty of
" flowers of every tint gladden the eye. What
" would have been thought of the propriety of
" placing a hundred bright and cheerful objects,
" suggestive of peace and happiness, in the ante-
" room to the torture chamber of the inquisition?
" It deserves to be noted that man, the only
" animal that laughs, has of all animals, according
" to the popular theory, least cause to laugh."—
Errors and Terrors, p. 64.

But there is much to be said beyond remarking on our natural thirst for joy and happiness, and the difficulty of explaining why it was ever implanted in man, except with a design that it should one day be gratified, fully and freely. There is this to be said, there is stored in every man a vast possibility of growth, of expansion in every direction, mental and intellectual, no less than spiritual. There are almost infinite germs in man, so to speak, capacities of every sort, latent as yet, but capable of a development, perhaps practically boundless, stored now up within us: they are perhaps unsuspected by the majority, and it is only at intervals, and as it were by chance, that we gain a passing glimpse at them. But undoubtedly they exist, and their existence, like that of all other natural facts, requires an explanation. *Why* do they exist—who planted within us these powers, and for what end? And they have been given to *all*, not to the good merely, but to man as man. I cannot but see in the very fact of their existence a silent prophecy, an intimation that the spark shall not be quenched in any case. Are they not a very message to man from GOD, a *hint*, eloquent by its very silence, eloquent and instinct with hope?

Consider next how strongly the analogy of nature, which is after all a very real revelation of GOD, bears against the popular view, which limits to the few moments of our present life all our chances of discipline, amendment, probation, and that though " all reason, all experience, all scrip-
" ture, unite in this, that the Divine work of
" teaching goes on behind, as well as before, the
" veil." See to what your creed really amounts.

You contradict all that we know of GOD's ways from every channel, in teaching that the mere fact of dying is the signal for a total change from all that has gone before. Consider this, and say whether any view which interposes so wide a gulf, as that commonly held does, between our present and our future life, can be true. In all GOD's dealings with us no sharp break intervenes between the successsive stages of life: each condition of being is developed out of a prior, and closely related stage. Now this being so, you ask me to believe that in another age all this is reversed, and that men with ample capacities for good still existing, are to be at one bound, consigned to outer darkness, to hopeless, endless torture. And the difficulty (surely an enormous one) of believing that a Parent will deliberately crush out all the lingering tendencies to good in HIS own children, is increased by the following consideration, viz :— that the whole of our human life here is so manifestly incomplete, so inchoate, that it has hardly afforded, in very many cases, a satisfactory probation, and in not a few cases, no probation at all.

This thought may be pursued further thus: an old proverb says very wisely, "the mills of "GOD grind *slowly*," and this Divine slowness or long-suffering is very conspicuous in GOD's ways. How slowly has HE been fitting this earth for man's habitation, and by what a long continued succession of stages, age succeeding age. At length man steps on the earth. Now, is all the Divine slowness to be at once changed—and why should it be? Man is to live for ever and ever : we are apt to forget what this means, and how altogether impossible it is to assign any proportion between the fleeting moments of earthly life, and the eternity that stretches away for ever and ever. If we compare a human life of average duration to one second of time, and compare eternity to the aggregate of all the seconds that have passed since time was, and that shall pass while time endures, still we assign to human life a proportionate duration infinitely too long. Now am I to believe that the same GOD who expends hundreds of thousands of years, in slowly fitting this earth for man's habitation, will only allow to man a few fleeting years, or months, or hours, as it may be, as his sole preparation time for eternity. To settle questions so unspeakably great in their issue, questions, stretching away to a horizon so far distant, that no power of thought can follow them, in such *hot haste*, does seem quite at variance with our Heavenly Father's ways, with all HE has shewn us of HIS modes of acting. Besides, do but look at the world : far the larger part of its population has not even heard of JESUS CHRIST. Are they —these untold myriads of myriads of hapless creatures—first to hear of CHRIST at the Day of Judgement?

Finally we pass to Holy Scripture. Here we

are at once confronted by a difficulty, so grave, that I confess, it to me seems quite decisive against the popular view. This difficulty is, that you are thus forced absolutely to *ignore*, to *suppress* a very large part of the Bible: a very numerous class of passages which clearly hold out a promise of universal restitution, or at least imply a destinct hope for all men. The view generally held is, in short, one-sided, and therefore wholly unfair: it is as though a judge should base a decision of the most weighty importance on one set of witnesses merely, neglecting the others who testify in a directly opposite sense. "Only "imagine the book of nature being studied in "this way, with one class of facts systematically "ignored; with one law, say of gravitation, fully "laid down, while the opposite law of centrifugal "motion was altogether overlooked, what results "in science could follow from such a method? "Yet this is the way in which not a few yet read "the Scriptures, taking their first partial sense "readings for the truth, and shutting their eyes "to all that the same Scripture testifies on the "other side."—*Catholic Eschatology Examined*, JUKES, p. 14.

An interesting illustration of the fact that the New Testament is *full* of passages teaching the larger hope, is furnished by the undoubted, but often unperceived, occurence over and over again, in the works of those who hold the popular creed, of language, which if fairly understood, imports the salvation of all men. This no doubt arises from the fact that phrases are used freely, while a traditional creed does, as so often, blind men to the real force of the expressions they employ— blind them in fact to everything outside the line of thought, which they are taught to believe constitutes the truth. Perhaps the best illustration that can be given of what I mean, will be gained by quoting from some collection of popular Hymns. I take then the well-known Hymns *Ancient and Modern*, and quote a few passages as instances of my meaning. Hymn 45 has this verse :—

> "Thou, sorrowing at the helpless cry,
> "*Of all creation* doomed to die,
> "Did'st save our lost and guilty race."

But this is universal salvation : *the race of man saved*, if words have any meaning. And this thought—the race saved—finds frequent expression elsewhere in these Hymns ; nor let any man who regards honesty of speech, and common *truthfulness*, say that to offer salvation merely, is, or can be, the same thing as to save. See Hymns 56, v. 3, 4, 5, 6 ; 57, v. 3 ; 62, v. 2, 6 ; 200, v. 6, etc. Again, listen to these solemn words and tell me what they mean. Hymn 97, Part 2, v. 2 :—

> "Precious flood which all creation,
> "From the stain of sin *hath freed.*"

And again v. 5 :—

> "That a shipwrecked race for ever
> "Might a port of refuge gain."

And Hymn 103, v. 5 :—

> "So a ransomed world shall ever
> "Praise THEE its redeeming LORD."

Can it be right to talk of a ransomed world for ever praising its Redeemer, and yet to mean that all the time the world is not actually ransomed, and perhaps half, perhaps more, of its population are groaning in endless pain? Is this consistent with truth? Again, other Hymns call on all creation to sing GOD's praise. Shall this praise then echo from Hell? See as a specimen, Hymns 144, v. 3 and 6, and 299, v. 4, etc., etc. I might well quote, in proof of this address to *all* creation to praise GOD, the familiar Doxology, but I will only notice here a well-known Hymn, No. 222 :—

> "O day for which *creation*,
> "And *all* its tribes were made;
> "O joy for all its former woes,
> "A thousand times repaid."

Now I will simply ask what these words mean: *all* creation is to have *all* its woes a thousand times repaid: if this is not universalism, what is universalism? Again, over and over, CHRIST is said to have vanquished sin, death, and SATAN :— Hymns 147, v. 2; 148, v. 2; 196, v. 3, etc. But how can this be true on the popular creed? To say that sin is vanquished, and death and SATAN, while Hell receives its myriads of the lost, is worse than absurd, *e.g.*, take this line from Hymn, No. 196 :—

> "Death of death, and Hell's destruction,"

and say if the universalist's creed could be more

distinctly stated: his utmost hopes have never gone beyond a vision of death abolished, and Hell destroyed? To pursue this further is needless, though it would be easy, and indeed full of interest: but I may point out how significant it is to find the very opponents of the larger hope *forced*, unconsciously, to employ language directly teaching universal salvation. The explanation is simply, that they have been using the words and ideas of Scripture, while the fair, honest meaning of their own words is obscured for them by the spell of a narrow traditional creed.

I can only permit myself a momentary allusion to another highly important class of passages, which are quite meaningless on the popular view —those which teach the doctrine of "the ages," and which, though obscured, unfortunately by our version, are yet really a very prominent feature in the teaching of the New Testament, as I hope to shew in a later chapter. But there are, apart from all these passages, certain tendencies in the Gospel, whose drift and character are impossible to mistake. That these tendencies exist I am far more certain than I can be of the meaning of any number of highly figurative texts. Now these tendencies are too clear, too broad, too distinct, to be considered accidental. So far from being a product of the age in which the New Testament was written, they are in conflict with the spirit of that age, and in advance of it. They must therefore represent something inherent in the Author of Christianity, and something essential to His design. I put the case very moderately in saying how extremely difficult it is to reconcile the popular creed with these undoubted tendencies of the New Testament. Can I reasonably believe that a system which beyond all other creeds has been distinguished by promoting mercy, goodness, love, tenderness for body and soul; a system, of which these qualities are the very essence, does indeed teach a doctrine of punishment so shocking, so horrible, that if really believed, it would turn this earth into a charnel-house, and spread over all nature lamentation, mourning, and woe?

Let me next shew that certain great principles of Revelation conflict with the popular creed. "I am sure" says a thoughtful writer, "these "are the two fundamental features of the "Christian Revelation, of which all its utterances "are the manifold expression, viz:—

"1.—The Parental Love of the Father.

"2.—The Solidarity of mankind to be "conformed to the image of His Son."—*Letters from a Mystic*, p. 169.

1.—No one can deny that the New Testament contains a special revelation of the parental tie uniting us to GOD. When ye pray, say, "our "Father;" these two words convey the spirit of the whole Gospel. Now it is not too much to assert that the view generally held is an absolute negation of all that the parental tie implies. It robs the relation of all meaning. It reduces to a simple mockery the Divine Fatherhood, though that is of the very essence of Christianity.

I repeat, the essence of Christianity perishes in the virtual denial of any true fatherhood of our race on GOD's part. Follow out this thought, for it is of primary importance. We lose sight of the value of the individual soul when dealing with the countless millions who have peopled this earth, and have passed away. What is one among so many? we are tempted to say, forgetting that the value of each human being is not in the least thereby altered: each soul is of infinite value as if it stood alone, in the eyes of GOD its Father. And more than this, are we not altogether apt to forget another vital point, to forget whose the loss is, if any one soul perishes? it is the man's own loss, says our popular creed. But is this all? No, a thousand times no! It is GOD's loss: it is the Father who loses HIS child. The straying sheep of the parable is the Great Shepherd's loss : the missing coin is the owner's loss. In this very fact lies the pledge that HE will seek on and on till HE find it. For think next of the value HE sets on each soul. HE has stamped each with HIS own image: has conferred on each a share of HIS own immortality—of Himself: do but realize these things; put them into plain words, till you come thoroughly to believe them, and you must see how impossible it becomes to credit that unworthy theology, which tells you that such a Father can ever let perish the work of HIS own fingers, HIS own offspring. One step further to make this clearer : how has HE shewn HIS sense of the value of the human spirit ? The Incarnation must say. It is human life taken into closest alliance with the divine, man and GOD meeting in the GOD-MAN. And then follows the Atonement, proof on proof of the same truth, when HE tasted death for every man, HE in whose death *all* died. Such is the chain, whose golden links I have been endeavouring to follow and trace, whose links bind to the Father above *every human soul* ; every human soul, be it, distinctly affirmed. Or stay, is there not yet wanting the final link to complete this chain ? It is to be found in the great truth, which completes what I have been saying ; the truth of the Oneness of the human race, its organic unity. Let us consider this.

2. This principle of the Oneness of our race is very legible in the divinely-given symbolism of the old law, and is reflected in the gospel with perfect clearness. What but this is the teaching of the "first-fruits," and the "first-born" in Scripture? These imply and include, the one, the *whole* harvest ; the other, the *whole* family, and not less. Now CHRIST is the " first-fruits."—1 *Cor.*, xv, 23, and CHRIST is the " first-born."—*Col.* i, 18. And what follows let St. PAUL say, " If the first-

"fruit be holy the lump is also holy," the whole race. Thus this principle is affirmed in the great central doctrine of the Incarnation. For in CHRIST the first-fruits, mankind, *i.e.*, the aggregate of humanity, is taken into GOD. And so in His death *all* died, as the New Testament assures us; and equally in HIS resurrection *all* rise, nay, are risen. In other words, CHRIST's relation as the second ADAM is not to individuals, but to the race, further it is an actual, not a possible or a potential relation, an *actual* relation giving salvation to all. "Once introduce the belief in CHRIST's
" divine nature, and HIS death and resurrection
" are no longer of the individual, but of the race.
" It was on this belief that the Church was founded
" and built up. The belief was not indeed drawn
" out with exact precision, yet it was always
" implied in the relation, which the believer was
" supposed to hold toward GOD. The formula of
" Baptism, which has never changed, is unintellig-
" ible without it. The Eucharist is emptied of the
" blessing which every age has sought in that
" Holy Sacrament, if it be taken way. If CHRIST
" took our nature upon HIM, as we believe, by
" an act of love, it was not that of one, but of all.
" HE was not one man only among men, but in
" HIM *all humanity are gathered up:* and thus
" now as at all time, *mankind* are, so to speak,
" *organically united with Him.*"—WESTCOTT, *Gospel of the Resurrection*, p. 176. And this it is, I think, this union of the race of man with HIMSELF, that JESUS CHRIST would teach in one of

His many *pregnant hints*, by always speaking of HIMSELF in HIS redeeming work, as the Son, not of the Jew, not of the Gentile, not of Mary, not of the Carpenter, but the Son of Man.

Yes, the Oneness of mankind is a principle that from the fall to the story of the Incarnation, runs through the texture of Holy Scripture. Have you ever quietly thought over the very strange fact of what is called original sin? Have you asked yourself what it means, that you are suffering for something done thousands of years before your birth? The questions raised by this enquiry we need not try to settle, but we may say that it means at least this, the organic unity of mankind; that mankind is not a collection of separate units, but an organised whole. Each individual is not, so to speak, complete in himself, but is a living stone in the great building, is a member of one great body, a member that if withrawn, there would ensue a distinct loss to the whole, a mutilation in fact of the body. And so ADAM'S sin sent a shock through the whole body, exactly as when a hurt to any part sends a shock through our present body. This is the painful side, but *it is only one side*; and unfortunately the popular creed, as so often, persists in looking at one side only, and that the dark side, and in looking away from the bright side, or at least in so looking at it as to miss its real aspect. But here the New Testament comes to our rescue and assures us that " if in ADAM *all* die, so in the "second ADAM *all* shall be made alive." The race is fallen; true, but the race is risen; quite as true. Both facts strictly correspond;

> "Of two such lessons why forget
> "The nobler and the Christlier one?"

A partial salvation is thus in absolute conflict with this fundamental principle which the fall affirms, and to which the Incarnation testifies; the unity of mankind, its Oneness. A partial salvation is in direct opposition to the great truth put by St. PAUL so clearly, that I never read his words without a feeling of wonder that any doubt can exist on this head. "If through the "offence of one (the) many be dead, much more "the grace of GOD, and the gift by grace, which "is by one man, JESUS CHRIST, hath abounded "unto (the) many * * as by the offence of one, "judgement came upon all men to condemnation, "even so by the righteousness of one, the free "gift came upon all men unto justification of "life." Observe, the offence is a thing actually imparted to, actually staining, ruining all men. And JESUS CHRIST came to bring to every man, to humanity, a salvation which shall be to mankind *much more* than the fall. But the popular view reads *much less*, and in millions of cases as much less as Hell is less than Heaven.

But again, the view generally held conflicts with another great principle, viz :—the unchangeableness of GOD. "If GOD be unchangeable then "what we see of HIM at any moment must be

"true of HIM at every moment of time, true of
" HIM also both before and after all the moments
" of time ; always and forever true of HIM. If
" HIS purpose be to save mankind, that purpose
" stands firm for ever, unaffected by man's sin,
" unshaken by the fact of death, unaltered and
" unalterable by men, by angels, by ought con-
" ceivable."—*Salvator Mundi*, p. 158. Redemption
is no after-thought, it was planned in the full
knowledge of all the extent of man's sin, knowing
all, GOD declared his purpose to be to save the
race. Redemption then is something indefeasible,
except indeed GOD can change, or man be
stronger than GOD, or the will of the created
stronger than the will of the Creator. " The
" gifts and calling of GOD are without repen-
" tance." —*Rom* xi, 29. That is, what GOD gives
cannot be refused, whom GOD calls they must be
saved. And this unchangeable purpose of GOD
is stated afresh in the words that describe JESUS
CHRIST as "*the same* yesterday, to-day, and for
" ever " (for the ages). Words deeply significant, and yet, whose true teaching so very often
escapes attention.

And here let me close this part of my argument by introducing a story, for whose truth I
vouch, to show how practical these considerations
really are. In a certain quarter of London one of
the many Evangelists, employed for that purpose,
had gone forth to preach to the people. When
he had concluded an eloquent address, he was

thus accosted by one of his hearers:—"Sir," said the man, "may I ask you one or two ques-"tions?' 'Surely," said the Preacher. "You "have told us, that GOD's love for us is very "great and very strong.' 'Yes.' 'That HE "sent HIS SON on purpose to save us, and that I "may be saved this moment if I will.' 'Yes.' "But, that if I go away without an immediate "acceptance of this offer, and if a few minutes "after I were to be, by any accident, killed on "my way home, I should find myself in Hell for "for ever.' 'Yes.' 'Then," said the man, "if "so, I don't want to have anything to do with "a Being *whose love for me can change so completely* "*in five minutes.*"

"WHAT THE CHURCH TEACHES."

"Proinde universos quidem salvat."—ST. CLEMENT of Alexandria, *Fragm. in I Joan.*

"O merciful GOD who hast made all men, and hatest nothing that
"THOU hast made; nor willest the death of a sinner   *   *   *
"Have mercy upon all Jews, Infidels, and Heretics,   *   *   *
"and so fetch them home, blessed LORD, to THY fold, that they
"may be saved among the remnant of the true Israelites."—*Good Friday Collect.*

"Valde alienum est ab Eo, ut ullam rationalem creaturam penitus
"perire sinat."—BOS. "Non potest aliter putare cor rationale."—
ST. ANSELM. *Cur Deus Homo*, ii, 4.

"O GOD, whose nature and prosperity *is ever* to have mercy and
"to forgive."—*Book of Common Prayer.*

CHAPTER IV.

"*WHAT THE CHURCH TEACHES.*"

In this chapter I propose to consider what the teaching of the Church really is on the subject of future punishment (including a review of our own Book of Common Prayer). Before attempting this, let us for the sake of greater clearness, sum up shortly the various arguments which have been occupying us in the two preceding chapters, and which, as I believe, shew how completely untenable is the popular view of future punishment—even without considering the vast body of direct Scriptural evidence to the same effect which I shall quote in later chapters.

First then, we have seen how it has pleased GOD to put within us a revelation of HIMSELF, in our moral nature, and we find it impossible to reconcile this HIS revelation, nay, HIS primary revelation, with the dogma of an endless Hell. We have been reminded how self-contradictory it is to assign to GOD, acts which the worst human being would not commit, and yet in the same breath to call HIM good. In the fact of the terrible solemnity, danger, and awe, that surround human life, we read a proof that a good Being would not have bestowed such a gift on man, whether he will or will not, except with an undoubted purpose that it should end in good. Further, we assert that the popular creed is wholly incredible because it involves the final triumph of evil over good; while it is also fairly open to the grave charge of producing a widespread unbelief, by the shock it gives to the human conscience, nay, of producing more scepticism than any other cause has ever done. Again, it has been pointed out that it is palpably unjust to assign to finite sin an infinite penalty: and attention has been directed to the tendency of the popular creed to promote a spirit of cruelty in human legislation, and in manners generally, and indeed to lower the moral tone all round, wherever it is received. It has been also shewn how extremely difficult it is to form any conception of the redeemed in Heaven as enjoying their own bliss, while conscious of the torment of the damned; while it is at least equally difficult to imagine them ignorant of it. Further, I have shewn that the popular creed really tends to make men tolerant of sin, because it teaches men to look on sin as a thing GOD will tolerate for ever in HIS universe. Again, the impossibility has been dwelt on of reconciling the popular view with what reason and Scripture teach, as to the nature and end of punishment, a point which really goes to the centre and core of this whole question. It has been shewn that a penalty, which is only vindictive, and has no higher end, is mere barbarism. I have also pointed out the absurdity of the supposition that GOD—considered simply as Almighty—can have put forth such efforts to rescue mankind and yet have failed, as the creed generally held represents HIM to have done; and that, though HE exerted HIS utmost strength, as is evidenced by HIS not sparing HIS own Son. Lastly, has been shewn the utter unreasonableness of asking others to accept a view of future torments as endless, which its warmest defenders shew by their own acts, that they do not themselves believe; because they in fact find it practically incredible.

Grave and weighty as the foregoing arguments are, they are not nearly all the preliminary considerations that can be urged against the popular view, and I shall now briefly sum up the further proofs contained in chapter iii. The first point alluded to has been the practical impossibility of dealing fairly with the mass of human beings on the ordinary view; because the *vast majority* are too good for Hell, and not good enough for Heaven. Another plea against the ordinary creed has been drawn from that natural and universal instinct which everywhere connects with ideas of joy the marriage day, and the hour of birth, and has been argued that GOD, in giving this instinct universally, cannot have intended to raise hopes which HE does not design fully to satisfy. A similar argument has been drawn from the natural and spontaneous thirst for happiness which GOD has planted within every man; and also from the fact—that there are latent in man vast capacities—which surely implies an intention to develop them one day. Attention has next been called to the difficulty of reconciling the view generally held, with the analogy of nature and of GOD's way of working, a point which a thoughtful mind can follow out in many ways. Passing to Holy Scripture, a difficulty of the very gravest kind has been shewn to exist, because the popular creed does *absolutely reject* the plain statements of a very large class of passages, which teach the salvation of all men: of this full proof will be given, as befits its importance, in the chapters that are to follow. Meantime, as illustrations of the fact that these passages do exist in the Bible, quotations have been given from Hymns, which though written by opponents of the larger hope of salvation, do yet in fact unconciously express that hope very clearly; because steeped in Scriptural phraseology, and imbued with its spirit. Again, it has been remarked that the popular creed directly conflicts with the admitted tendencies of the New Testament towards love and tenderness. Again a *fundamental* opposition has been pointed out between a partial salvation and the great principles revealed in Scripture, of the Divine Fatherhood and the Solidarity of mankind. The former principle is obviously sacrificed by the popular view, which robs it of all meaning. The latter principle, though not so generally recognised, is yet a fundamental principle of Scripture, is implied in every part of its teaching, *e.g.*, by the doctrines of the Fall of man, of the Incarnation, and of the Atonement. These all do recognise the organic unity of the race: but this unity is in direct conflict with a partial salvation. Finally, it has been shewn that the Divine unchangeableness is impeached by the ordinary creed, for GOD having once planned the world's salvation, HIS plan and counsel cannot change, but stand for ever good, unchanging as HE is without change.

Having thus concluded our summary, let us— before we turn to Holy Scripture and examine its teachings as to the future life—as it were pause on its threshold, and enquire what the teaching of the Church may be. And first, in the very term "Catholic," I cannot but find a significant lesson, in this very term which the Church has chosen to designate her mission. For what do these pages plead, but for the truest and widest catholicity of the Church of GOD, for a catholicity of salvation, an Incarnation which shall indeed mean the taking, not of some men, but of the manhood, the race, into GOD—for an atonement so wide, so effectual, so catholic, that no human sin shall escape, no guilt defeat its power to save. Indeed, as a thoughtful writer already quoted says, " until the Christian religion

"is posited on universal being, and that the
"calling of certain members into light or glory
"is for the well-being of the whole, its catholicity
"is a fiction." I think most readers are not aware how very widely the hope of the salvation of all men was held in the primitive church. Those who believed and taught it, more or less openly, or held kindred views, were among the most learned, the most eminent, and the most holy of the Christian Fathers. Passages to this effect may be found in the writings[*] of S. CLEMENT of Alexandria; S. AMBROSE; S. GREGORY of Nazianzus; S. GREGORY of Nyssa. Other names that may be cited as holding the same views are, DIODORUS of Tarsus, tutor of S. CHRYSOSTOM; THEODORE of Mopsuestia; THEOPHILUS of Antioch, 168, A.D.; ATHENAGORAS, 177, A.D. To these must be added the great name of the saintly ORIGEN, perhaps intellectually the greatest of the Fathers; as was JOHN SCOTUS ERIGENA probably the greatest of the Schoolmen; and both uncompromising advocates of the salvation of all men. "It "would seem, thus, that three at least of the "greatest schools of ancient Christian theology— "those of Alexandria, Antioch, and Cesarea— "leaned, on this subject, to the views of ORIGEN,

---

[*] The doctrine of *Reserve*, widely held at this time, probably at once restrained many from openly avowing their acceptance of the doctrine of the final salvation of all men, and also explains why others of the Fathers wrote at times with apparent inconsistency on this subject.

"in favour of the salvation of all men; not in their details, but in their general hopefulness."—*Mercy and Judgement*, p. 226. I append a few extracts to shew how these Fathers taught in the early centuries.

S. CLEMENT of Alexandria writes, "so HE saves *all men*. Some HE converts by penalties, others who follow HIM of their own will and in pursuance of the worthiness of HIS honour; that every knee may be bent to HIM, of those in Heaven, on earth, and under the earth; that is angels, men, and souls, who before HIS coming passed away from this mortal life."—*Adumb. in* 1 *ep. S. Joann.* These are words which speak for themselves. Again S. IRENÆUS, writing in the second century, has the following, "wherefore HE also drove him out of Paradise and put him far from the tree of life, not grudging him the tree of life, as some presume to say, but *taking pity on him*, that he might not continue always a transgressor; and that the sin which was in him might *not be immortal*, and the evil *interminable* and *irremediable*."—*Contr. Hær.* iii, c. 23.

S. GREGORY of Nyssa, in a remarkable passage, speaks of CHRIST as "both freeing *mankind* from their wickedness, and healing the *very inventor of wickedness*, (the Devil).—*Catech. Orat.* tom., iii, chap. 26. See how wide and distinct and uncompromising these words are; and yet many people speak of the dogma of universal salvation as a modern novelty. Again, in another treatise, the same great Father writes thus, "for it is "needful that at some time *evil shall be removed* "*utterly* and *entirely* from the realm of existence. "For since by its very nature evil cannot exist "apart from free choice, when all free choice "becomes in the power of GOD, shall not evil "advance to *utter abolition, so that no receptacle for* "*it shall be left.--De Anima et Resurrect.* tom. iii, p. 227, ed. Paris. Here you observe that the saint anticipates the utter extinction of evil at some future day. Again, writing on *Phil.* ii, 10, S. GREGORY says that "in this passage is sig- "nified, that when *evil has been obliterated* in the "long circuits of the œons, nothing shall be left "outside the limits of good ; but even from them "shall be unanimously uttered the confession of "the Lordship of CHRIST.*—De Anima et Resurrect.*, opp. i, ed Paris.

Another early Father writes thus, " and GOD "shewed great kindness to man, in this, that HE "did not suffer him to continue being in sin for "ever ; but as it were by a kind of banishment "cast him out of paradise, in order that, having "by punishment expiated within an appointed "time the sin, and having been disciplined, he "*should afterwards be recalled.* * * * Further "just as a vessel, when on being fashioned, it has "some flaw, is re-moulded, or re-made, that it "may *become new and entire* ; *so also it happens to* "*man by death.* For he is broken up by force, "that in the resurrection he may be found *whole,* "I mean righteous, spotless and immortal. — THEOPHILUS of Antioch, *ad Autolycum,* ii, 26.

I shall close this list with a passage, very distinct in its teaching of the larger hope. It really expresses the opinions of a remarkable woman S. MACRINA, sister of S. GREGORY of Nyssa, and is taken from the same book *De Anima,* p. 852, of S. GREGORY, which has been quoted above. " The word seems to lay down " the doctrine of the *perfect obliteration of wicked-* "*ness,* for if GOD shall be in all things that are, " obviously wickedness shall not be in them." These words are a comment on 1 *Cor.,* xv, 28, which speak of the time yet to come when GOD shall be "all in all," words which to those early saints conveyed a distinct impression that all evil would be obliterated.

And here I desire you to remark, when you read these opinions of the Fathers, in order rightly to estimate their weight, that they were written in an age when the very idea of mercy, as we now conceive it, was wholly unknown. Penalties were of every day occurrence then, that would now send a thrill of utter horror through the whole civilised world if inflicted in any one case; if indeed the details could be printed at all. Now when men living amidst these horrors— familiar with them all their lives, and accepting them as part of the order of things—found it yet impossible to believe in an endless Hell, we may well hail with pleasure their testimony. For in their case it was no mere sentimentalism, no exaggerated tenderness—such feelings were in that age impossible—that led them to proclaim the salvation of all men. It was merely the strength of their conviction that the gospel meant what it promised—life to the world. It was their deep abiding persuasion of the victory of JESUS CHRIST, and of its completeness. They so taught because they gathered from the very spirit of the gospel and from its letter—its distinct and repeated promises—as I hope to shew, a certainty, that the empire of CHRIST was destined to embrace all creation.

Nor is this all. Most deeply *significant* is it that these opinions * were held without the least consciousness on the part of these Fathers, that in so teaching they were deviating into the bye-paths of new or strange opinions. "For express-

---

* It is also important to bear in mind that the early Fathers held, almost unanimously, the doctrine of an intermediate state after death. Thus, e.g., so far from believing what our popular creed now teaches, let us hear JUSTIN MARTIN saying, "those who talk of their "souls going straight to Heaven after death are not Christians, or "even Jews."—*Dial.* These Fathers were practically unanimous in believing in a work of purification going on after death, a sort of cleansing fire (not the Roman Catholic Purgatory, which is a later and quite distinct belief). I call attention here to all this, because it is essential that we should learn how unfounded is our modern notion that death terminates our chances of spiritual growth, and amendment, and discipline.

"ing this hope, or this doctrine, they were never "abused, never attacked, never censured, *never* "*so much as challenged.* They lived, and they "died, and they have continued in the odour of "sanctity. They are recognised as Saints and "Fathers to this day." Nay, St. GREGORY of Nyssa, the most outspoken of them all, was mainly the author of the final clauses added to the Nicene Creed at the second General Council.

But notwithstanding this, the assertion is still repeated that the dogma of the final salvation of all men was condemned in the person of ORIGEN, at the fifth General Council. This assertion is, as will be shewn, distinctly untrue. An attempt was indeed made to procure a condemnation of this doctrine, but it completely failed. For a clearer understanding of the facts it must be premised that under the term "Origenism" were included very many speculative opinions of ORIGEN, *in no way whatever* necessarily connected with the belief in the final salvation of all men. "That belief was, in fact, widely held by those "who opposed ORIGEN in everything else." From this it follows that a condemnation of ORIGEN, or of "Origenism," would of itself prove *nothing* as to the condemnation of the doctrine of the final salvation of all men. On the whole I have thought it better for the avoidance of any doubt, instead of stating the case in my own words, to reproduce here an account of the whole matter from the pen of one whose competence will, I presume, not be questioned. It is right to add that some able critics dispute even the fact of the condemnation of ORIGEN (referred to below) at the fifth General Council, and produce reasons to show that his name was probably a later interpolation; but this is not material to the really important fact, which is, that neither the fifth nor any prior or subsequent General Council *has ever condemned the belief in the final salvation of all men, in the person of Origen, or of anyone else.*

"ORIGEN's opinion on the final restitution of
"all souls was especially disliked by the Emperor
"JUSTINIAN, and he caused the 'Home Synod'
"of Constantinople (*i.e.*, a committee of Bishops
"from a small number of sees near Constanti-
"nople, who, with some officers of the Metropoli-
"tan Church, formed a standing council for the
"Patriarch) to meet in 541, expressly to condemn
"this amongst other opinions of ORIGEN. The
"Synod passed fifteen canons, in which various
"theories of ORIGEN's were condemned, but
"*deliberately omitted* the particular one in
"question. Twelve years later the fifth General
"Council was assembled, and in one of its canons
"condemned ORIGEN by name amongst several
"others, but did not state what opinions of his
"were heretical; and as it was itself convened to
"discuss certain Nestorian views then current,
"no argument can be drawn from the business
"before it that it had this particular tenet in

WHAT THE CHURCH TEACHES. 77

"mind. The fifteen canons of the Home Synod "of 541 have been by some mistake included in "the decrees of the fifth General Council, but "even if the Council had adopted them as its own "(of which no probability exists), that would "leave the point in question untouched."

"The only shadow of ground for the current "impression on the subject is that the first of the "fifteen canons aforesaid of the Home Synod runs "thus: 'If any one should assert the fabulous "pre-existence of souls, and the monstrous resti-"tution which follows therefrom, let him be "anathema.' This can mean only that the "particular theory of restitution here specified is "condemned, and no other, so far as the canon is "concerned. But we learn what it was from the "fourteenth canon, which is as follows: 'If any "one shall say that in the future all rational "beings will form a single unit, personality and "number disappearing along with their bodies, "and that the ruin of the worlds and the putting-"off of the body will happen in virtue of know-"ledge of intellectual things, and also the loss of "[distinctive] names, and that there shall be an "identity of cognition and personality, and that "in this fabulous restoration they will be mere "naked spirits, as was the case in their fictitious "pre-existence, let him be anathema.' 'This is "decisive that the Synod took no account what-"ever of the Emperor's injunction to condemn "ORIGEN's denial of everlasting punishment, and

"thereby intended to leave it an open question."
—*Church Times*, Feb., 1884.

To the influence of St. AUGUSTINE, more than to any other single cause, is probably due the adoption of a harsher and narrower creed, by the Church in general, at a later day; and at a time when, it must be remembered, learning was dead and there prevailed in the Western Church, during many centuries, a wide-spread ignorance of the original languages of both the Old and New Testament. Combined with this ignorance there was also a general ferocity, and corruption of manners. Nor must we forget to state the important fact, that St. AUGUSTINE was himself imperfectly acquainted with Greek, having, as he confesses, shrunk from the toil of learning it thoroughly.—*Conf.* i, 14. And it is no disrespect to remark on the feebleness (and indeed vacillating character) of his arguments in consequence. Nor ought we to lose sight of the further fact, that the current belief, which grew up in later years, was so completely tempered by the doctrine of Purgatory (developed in these centuries) as to be for all practical purposes well nigh superseded.

But the earlier faith was by no means wholly dead. From amid the prevailing corruption and darkness, voices were still raised at intervals to proclaim the larger hope. A striking instance is that furnished by the case of

WHAT THE CHURCH TEACHES.

the famous JOHN SCOTUS ERIGENA, who in the ninth century, as the result of a careful study of the Greek Fathers, proclaimed *distinctly* the doctrine of universal salvation. Nor are later instances wanting. "Both St. THOMAS AQUINAS "and DURANDUS shew us that, even in their day, "absolute universalism was not unknown. It "was the opinion of the school of GILBERT of "Poictiers—St. THOMAS AQUINAS, *Sent.* iv, 45 "—and 'aliquorum juristarum'—DURANDUS."— *Mercy and Judgement*, p. 45. Again, a great name, St. ANSELM, in the twelfth century, writes thus: "It is quite foreign to GOD'S nature to "suffer any reasonable creature wholly to perish." — *Cur Deus Homo*, ii, 4. A striking proof of the survival of the earlier hope; "nor," adds the Saint, "is it possible for the reasonable mind to "think otherwise."

No doubt some will say: but does not the very fact that this belief in an endless Hell was permitted to spread so widely prove its truth? If so, I reply, why not then carry out your theory? Is transubstantiation true because it has prevailed so widely? Papal infallibility is a belief very widely spread; is it therefore to be accepted? The cultus of the Blessed Virgin is very wide spread; is it therefore Scriptural? Instances without end might be added. In fact, no more groundless belief can be pointed out than this, that the prevalence of an opinion is a proof of its truth. Are they who hold this strange opinion prepared to join the Church of Rome, and accept the supremacy of the Pope, because this belief is that of the vast majority of Christians in the Western Church? It has pleased GOD to permit in numberless cases error to prevail, and obscure in this present age His truth. . This very fact is but a louder call to us to work against all that hides or distorts that truth. Nay, it points not uncertainly to a conclusion in perfect agreement with the larger hope; this namely, that the present is but an initial stage of being; one of many ages, during which GOD is slowly, very slowly, working out a vast plan, and permits for a moment, as it were, an apparent triumph to error and to evil.

But in GOD's providence the true hope and faith of His Church has found expression in two documents, of an authority in its kind quite unique and fundamental; the two Creeds * the Apostle's, and that we call the Nicene. Rightly to estimate the weight of the testimony they bear, let us remember that in the second Great Ecumenical Council, where the Nicene Creed received its present shape, S. GREGORY of Nazianzus (whose opinions are above referred to) presided: while the chief author of the final

---

* Whatever we may think of the Athanasian Creed, when it speaks of "everlasting," that term can mean no more than the Scriptural *aionios*, which it represents, and as it is clear that everlasting is not the meaning of *aionios*, this creed is really quite consistent with the larger hope.

clauses, then added to the Creed, and ending with the significant words "I believe—in the life of the world to come," (in the *life*, be it remembered, and *in nothing more*) was S. GREGORY of Nyssa, whose words, quoted above, shew him to have been an unhesitating advocate of universal salvation. What can be more significant of the belief of the Church in these primitive days? Look at the facts. To a known believer in universal salvation is entrusted principally, by the Church, in her Great Council, the duty of defining the faith; and that definition runs thus: "I believe in the life of the world to come." And mark the position these words occupy in the creed (as does the corresponding clause in the Apostle's Creed). They close, and as it were, sum up the whole. The creed opens with a statement of belief in the Great Creator; it speaks of the Father, Son, and Holy Ghost: of the work of salvation, of the Incarnation, etc. But the great procession of the Christian verities ends, in both creeds, in the expressive assertion of *faith in everlasting life*. It is, as though both creeds proclaimed —that to this all Christian truth led, in this all Christian hope culminated. Do not fail, too, to remark the significant clause in the Nicene Creed, which tells us that, in Scriptural phrase, CHRIST's kingdom shall have *no end*. And again, remember how that most ancient Hymn, the *Te Deum*, declares that CHRIST took on HIM "to deliver man." But how man, *i.e.*, mankind is delivered, or CHRIST's kingdom has no end, while yet a Hell swallows up half the human race; that has never yet been explained.

Let us now pass on and see what our own Church teaches on this point. We shall I think find, if we examine it carefully, in our Book of Common Prayer—moulded as it is on primitive lines—not a few testimonies in favour of the larger hope. Go, for instance, into any of our Churches at the solemn service of Holy Baptism—what is the profession of faith required from the sponsors, how does it end? " Dost thou believe in everlasting life after death" and not a *word or hint further*. How suggestive, is it not? Again, in our Litany do we not pray that it may please GOD to have mercy, not on some men, but on *all men?* Is this not the larger hope? Do we not also address, in the same Litany, JESUS CHRIST as the " Lamb of GOD that taketh away the sins of the world," and that twice over? Do we not in Holy Communion repeat, *three* times in one prayer, this touching and truly Catholic address to CHRIST, as " taking away the sins of the "world?" And here it is right to ask, are words mere counters, a mere pretence, and that in our holiest moments? How does CHRIST *take away* the sins of the world, if to all eternity in Hell the sins of any men remain not taken away? On this point our Book of Common Prayer is specially emphatic, for in the proper preface for Easter-day we are bidden to remember how CHRIST "*hath taken away* the sins of the

"world; and has by HIS death *destroyed death.*"
But to abolish death in its Scriptural meaning is surely to abolish all that the Fall brought on man. Take next another instance: in one of her Ember-day Collects, the Church bids us thus pray: "To those who shall be ordained to any "holy function, grant Thy grace that they may "set forth Thy glory, and set forward the "salvation of all men." Does the salvation of *all* men mean the damnation of *most men*; of *any* man? Again I need not remind you how we pray "for all sorts and conditions of men; that "GOD's saving health may reach all nations." And so too when the Church bids us render thanks for a world redeemed, and for our creation, no less than for our redemption, how can this be if creation be not a certain promise of good? If creation does, as a matter of fact, imply an awful unutterable risk of Hell's torment, why bid a man give thanks for that which may be to him an occasion of endless pains? I will close this brief survey by reminding you of a fact, perhaps not always remembered, that our Church deliberately expunged that article of hers which (adopted in 1552) condemned the belief in the final salvation of all men.

"WHAT THE OLD TESTAMENT TEACHES."

"HE will not always chide, neither keepeth HE HIS anger for ever."—PSALM ciii, 9.

"HIS anger endureth *but a moment.*"—PSALM xxx, 5.

"From the time at which this great and far reaching promise or gospel was given to ABRAHAM, the universal scope of the Divine redemption is insisted on with growing emphasis, even in those Hebrew Scriptures which we too often assume to be animated only by a local and national spirit."—S. COX, D.D., *Salvator Mundi*, p. 177.

"As it is written in the book of ESAIAS the prophet saying:—Prepare ye the way of the LORD * * * Every valley shall be filled, and every mountain and hill shall be brought low * * * and *all flesh* shall see the salvation of GOD."—ST. LUKE, iii, 4-6.

"Who is a GOD like unto THEE, that pardoneth iniquity * * * HE retaineth not HIS anger for ever, because HE delighteth in mercy."—MICAH vii, 18.

CHAPTER V.

"*WHAT THE OLD TESTAMENT TEACHES.*"

In the last chapter I endeavoured to give you an outline of what the Church has taught on this subject. I trust it has been made clear that the belief in the final salvation of all men is no novelty, no modern brand-new doctrine; got up to meet the difficulties of a sentimental age. You have seen on the contrary, that this belief has found expression in the writings of many of the most eminent Fathers, especially the great Greek Fathers (whose authority would naturally be greatest on a question affecting the text of the New Testament) and that in the purest ages of the Church.* You have looked with me at the two Ancient Creeds, and have seen how suggestive is their testimony, especially when the facts are considered which I have given above, with regard to

---

* The popular view—though doubtless always held by some—did not become the general belief till an age of comparative darkness and ignorance had succeeded the days of the great Greek Fathers.

the Nicene Creed and the second General Council. "There is great significance," says an excellent authority, "in the fact that in the simplest of "our symbols; the Apostle's Creed; and in the "most universal of them, the Nicæno-Constantino- "politan we are called on to express our belief in "the life but not in the death to come."—Rev. Dr. LITTLEDALE, *Cont. Review.* You have been shewn that the attempt to procure the condemnation of ORIGEN's belief in the final salvation of all men *completely failed*, a fact ever to be borne in mind; and that the question remains, so far as Church authority is concerned, an open one to this day. Again, an examination of our own Prayer Book has shewn the larger hope for all men embodied there in various forms. It has found distinct expression in not a few parts of our Church's service, liturgy and prayers.

From the Church I next turn to the Old Testament. There, too, we shall find abundant, perhaps to many, unexpected confirmation of the larger hope, though I can merely attempt to give an outline, and that a brief one, of its teaching. True, in the Old Testament the promises are, it may be said, mainly temporal, but still we have unmistakeable evidence of a plan of mercy revealed in its pages, and destined to embrace all men. Nor need this interpretation of the older volume of GOD's word rest on mere conjecture: let me call as a witness, no less a person than the Apostle S. PETER. He shall tell us what the true teaching of the Old Testament on this subject is. The Apostle in one of the very earliest of his addresses, *Acts* iii, 21, takes occasion to explain the real purpose of GOD in JESUS CHRIST. There is to come finally a time of universal restoration, "restitution of *all* "things." He adds the significant words that GOD had promised this "by the mouth of all "HIS holy Prophets since the world began;" and therefore we who teach this hope are but following in the steps of all GOD's holy Prophets. Thus S. PETER would have us go to the Old Testament, and weave, as it were, its varied predictions into one concordant whole: gather its scattered promises till they with one voice proclaim the restitution of all things.

It is not my design minutely to consider the varied promises of blessing to all men contained in the Old Testament, though they can be traced almost everywhere. Thus with the promise to ABRAHAM was blended an intimation of blessing to the race of man; to all the families of the earth. And this intimation of a world-wide blessing, as has been often pointed out, grows more frequent as the stream of revelation flows on. " The Psalmists are full of the largest and " happiest forecasts. When they speak of the " coming Messiah, they are at the farthest from " claiming the blessings of HIS reign exclusively " for themselves; on the contrary, they say, ' HIS " name shall endure for ever: HIS name shall be

"continued as long as the sun; and men shall
"be blessed in HIM; *all* nations shall call HIM
"blessed'   *   *   * "They constantly breathe
"forth the invitation, 'O praise the Lord *all* ye
"nations; praise HIM *all* ye people."—*Salvator Mundi*, p. 178. Let me further instance such words as these, "unto THEE shall *all* flesh
": come." Other examples of the same address to all nations—to all peoples—bidding them join in GOD's praise, and surely anticipating that they would one day do so, are frequent in the Psalms. Take for example those our Prayer Book has made familiar, *e.g.*, *Cantate Domino*. It is not alone the house of Israel that shares GOD's mercy and truth, but *all the ends of the world* are declared to have seen the salvation of our GOD—see *Is.* xl, 5—and so in the next verse *all* lands are bidden to shew themselves joyful unto the Lord. To the same effect is the familiar clause of the Jubilate, "O be joyful in the Lord
"*all* ye lands." In fine, in this spirit the Psalter closes with the noble far-resounding strain, "let
"everything that hath breath, praise the Lord." In this universal hope is to be found the true spirit of the Psalmists, in these invitations addressed, not to Israel, but to all nations.

Of the greater Prophets the same is true; though I need not speak in detail of them. From amid their varied contents, at times break forth promises of the widest, amplest hope; anticipations of a time of universal bliss and joy, of a world in which all pain and sorrow shall have passed away. But these passages are in the main familiar to you, and I need hardly quote them. They have found their way to the heart of Christendom, and have stamped themselves on its literature. "Take however only this one "sentence from the evangelical Prophet, and "take it mainly because S. Paul echoes it back, "and interprets it as he echoes it. It is Jehovah "who speaks these words by the mouth of "Isaiah: 'Look unto me and be ye saved, all "ye ends of the earth; for I am God and there "is none other: I have sworn by myself and "the word is gone out of my mouth in righteous- "ness and shall not return, that unto me every "knee shall bend and every tongue confess.' "Could any words more emphatically declare "it to be the divine purpose that the *whole earth*, "to the very end of it shall be saved; that "every knee shall bow in homage before God, "and every tongue take the oath of fealty to "Him? Are we not expressly told that this "declaration, since it has come from the righteous "mouth of God, cannot return unto Him void, "but must accomplish its object; that object "being the salvation of the human race? St. "Paul echoes this great word in the epistle to "the Philippians, and though on his lips it gains "definiteness and precision, assuredly it loses no "jot or tittle of its breadth: he affirms, *Phil.* ii, "9-11, 'That God hath highly exalted Him, and "given Him a name which is above every name, "in order that at the name of JESUS every knee should bow;' "not only every knee of man — for now the promise grows incalculably wider— but 'every knee in Heaven and on earth, and under the earth : and that every tongue should confess that JESUS CHRIST is Lord, to the glory of GOD the Father.' "It is hard to understand ISAIAH as proclaiming less than a universal redemption, but if S. PAUL did not mean to proclaim a redemption as wide as the universe, what use or force is there in words?"—*Salvator Mundi*, p. 180.

And remember how full are the Prophets, and the Psalms no less, of pictures of the vastness of the divine mercy, of HIS tenderness that never fails. Even from amid the sadness of the *Lamentations* we hear a voice assuring us that "GOD will *not cast off for ever*, but though HE cause grief, yet will HE have compassion according to the multitude of his mercies."— Lam. iii, 31. Or take these words of ISAIAH: "I will not contend for ever, neither will I be *always wroth!* for the spirit should fail before me, and the souls which I have made."—*Isaiah* lvii, 16. This idea is a favourite one; the contrast between the short duration of GOD's anger and the enduring *eternal character of His love.* "So, in a little wrath I hid my face from thee for a moment, but with *everlasting* kindness will I have mercy on thee, saith the Lord thy Redeemer."—*Is.* liv, 8.

We have spoken of the pictures of universal blessedness that are to be found in the greater Prophets, " perhaps" says the author already quoted, " some of you may not be equally "familiar with the fact that these same pictures "are also to be found in the minor Prophets;" a fact very suggestive that " every one of these " brief poems, or collections of poems, has its tiny " Apocalypse. And mark this point well, while "each of the minor Prophets sees the vision " of a whole world redeemed to the love and " service of righteousness, this vision of redemp-"tion is invariably accompanied by a *vision of* "*judgement.*" The significance of this will be seen when we come in a later chapter (ch. ix) to discuss what the true meaning is of these divine judgements, which are too often regarded as merely implying God's wrath.

At least, if not all, yet very many of the minor Prophets do predict the coming of a time of universal redemption. So JOEL, ii, 28, tells of the spirit as being poured upon *all* flesh. HABBUKUK can look beyond the terrors of judgement and see the " *earth* filled with the "knowledge of the glory of the LORD, as the "*waters cover the sea.*"—ch. ii, 14. Is not this wonderful? Can you not enter into St. PETER'S words as he stood forth, while yet Christianity was scarcely born, to proclaim as its glorious aim and scope, the universal restoration—the paradise God regained for mankind—all things made new. (*Acts* iii, 21.)

But I resume. In ZEPHANIAH we read the same glorious prospect, the same universal hope. He speaks of GOD's judgements as being terrible to the nations, in order that "men may worship "HIM, *every one* from his place even *all the isles* "*of the heathen.*"—ch. ii, 11. And again, in the same Prophet, we are told how GOD is to send HIS fiery judgements to purify men, "that they "may *all* call upon the name of the LORD to serve "HIM with one consent" (ch. iii, 8-9). So MALACHI closes the prophetic line with an intimation indeed of judgement—of a refining fire—but together with this, nay in consequence of this, is the prospect unfolded, that from the "*rising of the sun* "*unto the going down of the same*, GOD's name "shall be great among the Gentiles, and in *every* "place incense and pure offerings shall be offered "to HIM" (chs. i, 11, and iii, 2-3).

Brief as the above survey has been, it has, I trust, served to indicate how, through all the Old Testament, the thread of *universal* hope runs: how the Prophets—Seers and Psalmists—of Israel did foreshadow a coming age; when sin should be no more, and sorrow and sighing should flee away for ever. To the New Testament I propose to devote an examination more in detail, as its great importance demands, in the next chapter.

"WHAT THE NEW TESTAMENT TEACHES."

"And here I may briefly say, that to my own mind, the language
"of the New Testament appears *unequivocally to affirm the redemption
"of all men;* their actual redemption from this evil and diseased state
"in which we now are; the actual raising up of all to a perfect life.
"To my own mind this *universality* seems to be clearly expressed in
"Scripture, and to give an unutterable delight to life."—JAMES
HINTON, *The Mystery of Pain*, p. 61.

"I have read most of the books on the theme discussed in this
"volume, which have appeared during the last half century * * *
"but on the whole I think I may say, quite simply and honestly,
"that I have got my views (in favour of a universal salvation) from
"long study of the New Testament itself, and not from any comment
"on it."—S. COX, D.D., preface to *Salvator Mundi*.

CHAPTER VI.

"*WHAT THE NEW TESTAMENT TEACHES.*"

We now turn to an examination of the very numerous passages in the New Testament which clearly declare, or imply, the salvation of all men: how numerous these are, how distinct their teaching, we shall see. One thing only I ask, which common fairness and honesty require, that our Lord and His Evangelists and Apostles may be understood to *mean what they say*. Thus, to take a few instances out of many: when they speak of all men I assume them to mean all men, and not some men; when they speak of all things I assume them to mean all things; when they speak of life and salvation as given to the world, I assume them to mean given, and not merely offered; when they speak of the destruction of death, of the Devil, of the works of the Devil, I assume them to mean that these shall be destroyed, and not preserved for ever in Hell; when they tell us that the whole of creation suffers but that it shall be delivered, I assume they mean an actual deliverance of all created things; when they tell us that Redemption is wider, broader, and stronger than the Fall, I assume that they mean to tell us at least this, that all the evil caused by the Fall shall be swept away; when they describe CHRIST'S empire as extending over all things and all creatures, and tell us that every tongue must join in homage to HIM, I assume them to mean what their words convey in their ordinary sense: if I did not, should I not, in fact, be making GOD a liar?

S. MATTHEW xviii, 2.

"FOR THE SON OF MAN IS COME TO SAVE THAT WHICH IS LOST."

Now the question is simply this, will JESUS CHRIST do what HE has come to do? Will HE save *the lost*, and not *some of the lost merely, a totally different thing*? How can "the lost" be saved, if countless myriads, as the popular creed teaches, shall be finally lost? nay, if any are finally lost, surely "the lost" are not saved.

S. MATTHEW xii, 32.

"AND WHOSOEVER SPEAKETH A WORD AGAINST THE SON OF MAN IT SHALL BE FORGIVEN HIM, BUT WHOSOEVER SPEAKETH AGAINST THE HOLY GHOST IT SHALL NOT BE FORGIVEN HIM, NEITHER IN THIS WORLD, NOR IN THE WORLD TO COME."

I cite this passage for the sake of the remarkable hint it conveys as to forgiveness in the world to come, a point of primary importance in opposing the popular creed. Let me quote here the words of an eminent Divine, Archbishop WAKE, who in his *Discourse of Purgatory*, p. 20, says, speaking of this future forgiveness in connection with the present passage, "It may "with much more agreement to the text follow "that *all men, be their sins what they may, shall* "*have grace of repentance, whereby they may be* "*pardoned in the world to come*, blasphemy against "the Holy Ghost alone excepted." Our version here, as so often, in rendering "age" by the incorrect term "world," has quite obscured the meaning. Scripture nowhere, I think, speaks of the present and the future world, as though there were but these two ; it tells us uniformly of a present "age" to which many "ages" are to succeed ; through all which the Divine plan in the work of Redemption is to go on. And even the mysterious sin against the Holy Ghost may, with perfect conformity to the present passage, find pardon, if not here or in the next age yet in some distant one.

S. MATTHEW xiii, 33.

"THE KINGDOM OF HEAVEN IS LIKE UNTO LEAVEN WHICH A WOMAN TOOK AND HID IN THREE MEASURES OF MEAL TILL THE WHOLE WAS LEAVENED."

Here is a passage which assuredly teaches a universal salvation. The kingdom of Heaven is set on this earth as leaven in meal ; and as the leaven works till the whole mass is leavened, so the Kingdom of Heaven is destined to leaven the whole earth, *i.e.*, to save all men. You cannot limit the "meal" of the parable in any way, it is the whole world that CHRIST claims as HIS kingdom ; of the world HE is the light, the life, the Saviour. All things are HIS and all souls (whether behind the veil or not), and all that CHRIST claims —"*the whole*"-- shall one day be leavened.

S. LUKE i, 33.

"OF HIS KINGDOM THERE SHALL BE NO END."

No end of HIS kingdom! but if there be a Hell full of souls finally lost, there would surely be an end to HIS kingdom, and this text could not be true. To assert for CHRIST a kingdom without any limit or bound, is plainly to teach a universal salvation.

S. LUKE iii, 5.

"ALL FLESH SHALL SEE THE SALVATION OF GOD."

Quoted from ISAIAH; he says, speaking of redemption, ch. xl, "*Every* valley shall be "exalted, and *every* mountain and hill shall be "made low, and the glory of the Lord shall be "revealed, and *all* flesh shall see it together." Can you fairly reconcile these words with a partial salvation ? Thus when the Prophet says in the same chapter, verse 6, "all flesh is grass," who doubts the universality of his words; and if so, is it not a violation of all fairness in an exactly parallel case, to doubt the universality of the salvation?

S. LUKE xii, 48.

"BUT HE THAT KNEW NOT, AND DID COMMIT THINGS WORTHY OF STRIPES, SHALL BE BEATEN WITH FEW STRIPES."

"This seems to prove that there is such a thing "in the life to come as a terminable retribution. "Can 'few' be synonymous with 'endless?'"— see *Mercy and Judgement*, p. 478. It has been pertinently asked "what is to be done (on the "popular view) with the man after the few stripes "have been inflicted?"

S. LUKE xv, 4.

"WHAT MAN OF YOU HAVING AN HUNDRED SHEEP IN THE WILDERNESS, IF HE LOSE ONE OF THEM DOTH NOT LEAVE THE NINETY AND NINE IN THE WILDERNESS AND GO AFTER THAT WHICH IS LOST UNTIL HE FIND IT?"

"Yes" says a writer already quoted, "as long "as there is one member of the race imperfect, "the shepherd parent is pursuing it in love until "it be safely rested on his shoulders; and all "the rest of mankind are crying out for the "missing member, without which their own life "does not fully or freely vibrate." See how broadly CHRIST puts this case. It was to *all* the *publicans and sinners*, v. 1, that HE was speaking, lest we might narrow HIS precious words to a few elect. And again see how broadly HE bases HIS argument, " what man of you," HE asks " would not do this ? " As though to assure us that in the common feeling of humanity, shared by even publicans and sinners, we have safe warrant to conclude that our Father will seek on and on till HE find *every* erring child. Lastly, note how the straying sheep is represented as being the shepherd's loss. When man strays GOD is the loser, and GOD in seeking man is trying to retreive HIS own loss, But how seldom is this weighty truth recognised ?

S. LUKE xv. 8.

"EITHER WHAT WOMAN HAVING TEN PIECES OF SILVER, IF SHE LOSE ONE PIECE, DOTH NOT LIGHT A CANDLE AND SWEEP THE HOUSE AND SEEK DILIGENTLY TILL SHE FIND IT ? "

Here is precisely the same broad human basis, and the same idea, the sense of loss is that of the owner, *i.e.*, GOD. Keep steadily in view three facts, which distinctly emerge from these parables : 1—our own feelings of love and pity are a safe guide to GOD's feelings ; " what man " of you ? " 2—every lost soul is GOD's loss, who therefore may be trusted to seek its recovery ; and 3—to seek *till He find it.*

S. LUKE xiii, 20-1.

"WHEREUNTO SHALL I LIKEN THE KINGDOM OF GOD? IT IS LIKE LEAVEN, WHICH A WOMAN TOOK AND HID, IN THREE MEASURES OF MEAL, TILL THE WHOLE WAS LEAVENED."

Till *the whole* was leavened, remember. Not till then shall the Kingdom of Heaven be complete; not till then the race redeemed shall have been leavened through and through.—See note on *S. Matt.* xiii, 33.

S. LUKE xix, 10.

"FOR THE SON OF MAN IS COME TO SEEK AND TO SAVE THAT WHICH WAS LOST."

If so, I gather from HIS own parables, and HIS essential nature, that so long as *any thing is lost*, JESUS CHRIST will go on seeking and saving; for is HE not always the same? "The lost" are HIS charge, and not some of the lost, a very different thing, as I have before said. Shall any thing separate any lost one from HIS love? Is HE not Lord of the dead as truly as of the living? Did HE not go from the bitter cross to the lost spirits in prison, to preach, as St. PETER tells us, the Gospel to *the dead*. And yet too many of us have been trained to think that death is so strong a thing, that it paralyses HIS power to save! We have not yet learned that all things— life and death, time and eternity—are in JESUS' hand. We have forgotten, apparently, that *all* power has been given unto HIM; that HE has the keys of death.

S. JOHN i, 7.

"THE SAME CAME FOR A WITNESS, TO BEAR WITNESS OF THE LIGHT, THAT ALL MEN THROUGH HIM MIGHT BELIEVE."

Yes, that *all* men might believe, that is indeed the Divine purpose—the purpose of HIM who sent the Baptist. But who is there that shall say, that what GOD purposes to do HE will fail to accomplish? I know that HE cannot fail: I read distinctly of the *immutability* of HIS counsel, of HIS purpose (*Heb.* vi, 17). Am I to believe that the immutable purpose of the unchanging GOD shall come to nothing?

S. JOHN i, 2-9.

"BEHOLD THE LAMB OF GOD WHICH TAKETH AWAY THE SIN OF THE WORLD."

I often ask myself, how could the extent of the work of CHRIST be more distinctly intimated. It is the world's sin, and not less, that HE takes away. But if it is *taken away*, how can there be an endless Hell for its punishment? Is all this mere playing with words? Have we come to asserting that of GOD's word?

S. JOHN iii, 17.

"FOR GOD SENT NOT HIS SON INTO THE WORLD TO CONDEMN THE WORLD; BUT THAT THE WORLD THROUGH HIM MIGHT BE SAVED."

Again the same plain statement, as to the *world's* salvation and GOD's purpose to save it; and again I ask, are we to believe GOD when

He tells us that His purpose in Redemption is the salvation of the world, and assures us by His Prophets that His word shall not return unto Him void, but shall accomplish that which He pleases.

S. JOHN iii, 35.

"THE FATHER LOVETH THE SON, AND HATH GIVEN ALL THINGS INTO HIS HAND."

The relevance of this is obvious, "*all* that the "Father hath given me," says CHRIST, "shall "come unto me," ch. vi, 37. It is one of the large group of passages showing the universality of CHRIST's Kingdom. Compare ch. xiii, 3, and see the connection of the gift of all things to CHRIST and His atoning death—very significant I think, and perhaps overlooked by many. Also see *S. Matt.* vi, 27, where just before the well-known appeal, " come unto me," JESUS has been saying that *all things* were delivered unto HIM by His Father; a connection surely suggestive. Read, too, in this light, *S. Matt.* xxviii, 18, and note the connection between all power claimed by CHRIST, and His claim to bring all nations to discipleship. So *Heb.* ii, 8-9, in this last passage again the connection between the gift of all things to JESUS CHRIST, and His atonement is very marked—His tasting death for *every* man. The Divine Son is set over all things; as He creates *all* things (actually) so He redeems and restores *all* things (actually, not potentially); His relation is to all, not a part.

GOD has given to HIM all things ; and all things given to HIM shall come to HIM. So says Holy Scripture, and the universalist is but accepting and believing what it says.

S. JOHN iv, 42.
"THIS IS INDEED THE CHRIST, THE SAVIOUR OF THE WORLD."

The same truth—the *world* saved. In saying GOD is the creator of the world, an actual creation is meant ; so in saying CHRIST is the Saviour of the world, not anything less than an actual salvation is meant ; a point I must be forgiven for pressing, so true is it and so generally forgotten.

S. JOHN vi, 12.
"GATHER UP THE FRAGMENTS THAT REMAIN, THAT NOTHING BE LOST."

In passing we may note this passage, for CHRIST's *hints* go very far, and are full of meaning. What is the larger hope but this, that of all that the Father hath given HIM HE will lose nothing ?

S. JOHN vi, 33.
"THE BREAD OF GOD IS HE WHICH COMETH DOWN FROM HEAVEN, AND GIVETH LIFE UNTO THE WORLD."

Here we are told that life is given, not offered merely, to the world. The world (*Kosmos*) is in Scripture the ungodly mass, the outer circle. It is contrasted with the inner circle of the faithful, the elect. But this *world* is over and over again claimed by CHRIST. HE saves it; HE gives life to it; HE gives light to it. Remember to " offer " is not the same as to " give."

S. JOHN vi, 37-9.

"ALL THAT THE FATHER GIVETH ME SHALL COME TO ME, AND HIM THAT COMETH TO ME I WILL IN NO WISE CAST OUT; FOR I CAME DOWN FROM HEAVEN NOT TO DO MINE OWN WILL, BUT THE WILL OF HIM THAT SENT ME. AND THIS IS THE FATHER'S WILL WHICH HATH SENT ME, THAT OF ALL WHICH HE HATH GIVEN ME I SHOULD LOSE NOTHING."

This is very explicit; we have seen that GOD the Father has given to CHRIST, not some things, but *all* things; and here we have the word and promise of JESUS CHRIST that, *all* that has been given to HIM shall come to HIM, and that nothing shall be lost (ch. vi, 12). What further is needed to prove from Scripture a universal salvation? What further could GOD possibly say?

S. JOHN vi, 51.

" MY FLESH WHICH I WILL GIVE FOR THE LIFE OF THE WORLD."

Again it is the *world* for whose life CHRIST is to give HIS flesh. Can HE give in vain? HIS gifts are " without repentance," *i.e.*, must be effectual. To say that HIS word can return to HIM having failed, or HIS gifts not take effect, is to contradict Holy Scripture.

S. JOHN viii, 12.
"Then spake Jesus again unto them, I am the light of the world."

Here, too, the *world*, the ungodly world, is that of which CHRIST is the Light as well as the Life.

S. JOHN ix, 5.
"When I am in the world, I am the light of the world."—*Rev. Version.*

The same idea over and over again; not the elect merely, but the *world*, enlightened; quickened; saved.

S. JOHN xii, 32.
"And I, if I be lifted up from the earth, will draw all men unto me."

One would expect that CHRIST's own words would be belived by those who teach in HIS name. I think the plainest comment the best here. A partial drawing, *i e.*, a partial salvation makes HIS words *untrue*. One reads* the comments of good men on this passage, with a feeling akin to despair, as they attempt to make JESUS CHRIST say that which HE did not say, and not say that which HE did say. It is only in reading such remarks of commentators that one realises

---

* Canon WESTCOTT is an honourable exception, who, in the *Speaker's Commentary*, says:—"The phrase must not be limited in "any way; we must receive it as it stands." Surely! but to receive it as it stands is to teach, in plain words, universal salvation.

the terrible power of an evil traditional creed to prevert the judgement, and to blind good men to the plainest teachings of the Bible—to its clearest promises of universal salvation !

S. JOHN xii, 47.

"FOR I CAME NOT TO JUDGE* THE WORLD, BUT TO SAVE THE WORLD."

This is as distinct as possible : its force can only be evaded by asserting that CHRIST will fail to accomplish that very thing which HE came to do : and this assertion must be made in the teeth of those repeated and explicit passages which declare the completion of HIS triumph—the endlessness of HIS kingdom.

I JOHN ii, 2.

"AND HE IS THE PROPITIATION FOR OUR SINS: AND NOT FOR OURS ONLY, BUT ALSO FOR THE SINS OF THE WHOLE WORLD."

Notice here the world contrasted with the true disciples ; and yet the propitiation is not to be confined to the few, it is for all. S. JOHN's anxiety is to *assert this for all*. Remember too, that here in whatever sense CHRIST is a propitiation for " our " sins, in the same sense HE is so for

---

* Of course the meaning is, that the work of JESUS CHRIST is the salvation of the world : the text cannot, in the face of numerous passages, intend to teach that JESUS does not judge ; in fact it is to the SON that judgement has been committed. But HE, by HIS judgements, saves (see Ch. ix, section on judgement).

the sins of the whole world. Here, as so often, the narrower and wider purposes of salvation are both mentioned : the narrower not excluding, as in the popular view, but *including* and *implying* the wider ; a truth of the deepest importance.

I JOHN iii, 8.

"FOR THIS PURPOSE THE SON OF GOD WAS MANIFESTED, THAT HE MIGHT DESTROY THE WORKS OF THE DEVIL."

Now who can read with impartial mind this explicit statement, and doubt its meaning ? The very purpose of the manifestation of GOD's Son is the sweeping away of Satan's works. How then can this *possibly be true*, while pain and sin and Hell endure for ever and ever ? No ideas can be more exactly opposed than the permanence of evil, and yet the destruction of the works of the Devil. Is sin the Devil's work ? Is all that sin involves the work of the Devil ? Yes, or No ? You cannot answer in the negative. But if the affirmative be true, then all is to be swept away ; Hell and sin and sorrow.

I JOHN iv, 14.

"AND WE HAVE SEEN AND DO TESTIFY, THAT THE FATHER SENT THE SON TO BE THE SAVIOUR OF THE WORLD."

Does it not savour of mockery to say that the Father sent the Son to destroy evil and to save the world, and yet that neither shall evil be destroyed or the world saved! And remember,

I am only pleading for CHRIST'S doing the very thing He has come to do, and promised to do.

REVELATIONS i, 18.
"I HAVE THE KEYS OF HELL AND DEATH."

Significant surely! How, if so, can death (the second, or any death) sever from JESUS CHRIST (*who holds the keys*), from HIS power to save? If this were only believed, what light (sorely needed) it would shed on the whole subject of death.—See on death in ch. ix.

REVELATIONS v, 13.
"AND EVERY CREATURE WHICH IS IN HEAVEN, AND ON THE EARTH, AND UNDER THE EARTH, AND SUCH AS ARE IN THE SEA, AND ALL THAT ARE IN THEM, HEARD I SAYING UNTO HIM THAT SITTETH ON THE THRONE, AND UNTO THE LAMB, BLESSINGS, ETC."

How comprehensive this picture! Its words embrace every created thing—on the earth, and under the earth, and in the sea. All are represented as swelling the chorus of praise to GOD, and to the Lamb. Yes, to such an ending we trust and hope that all creation is indeed coming, because we trust in the living GOD, who is the Saviour of all men and because we believe HIS own words that promise that all things shall be made new. Else, how could *all things* join in this glorious chorus? Note, too, how the story of salvation is here told, so to speak. It goes (as pointed out already, see *I John* ii, 2) from the *few* to the *many*. First, the elders, and the living creatures, raise the song of praise. They are said to be the redeemed out of every kindred and nation. Then is heard the voice of many angels, and lastly comes the turn of *every creature* which is in Heaven, and on the earth, and under the earth, to join in the strain of praise, which has now swelled so as to embrace the universe.

REVELATIONS xxi, 5.
"Behold I make all things new."

It is the same glorious hope, not for some, but for *all*, no less than *all things* are to be made new. Here again we have a universal restoration distinctly promised—the salvation of all.

REVELATIONS xxii, 2-3.
"And the leaves of the tree were for the healing of the nations. And there shall be no more curse."

Here is a striking hint—after the manner of the Scripture—as to a future work of restoration; a hint that the nations are one day to be healed; that in another age there shall be ministries of salvation; for all this is subsequent to the passing away of the present earth, and the present Heaven (ch. xxi, 1). And as a result of this healing, there shall be no more curse—no pain—no tears—and no endless Hell therefore, but *all things* made new.

ACTS ii, 17.

"AND IT SHALL COME TO PASS, SAITH GOD, I WILL POUR OUT OF MY SPIRIT UPON ALL FLESH."

This, and *no less*, is over and over again declared to be the scope and extent of CHRIST's Redemption. Compare these words, too, with the passages following, in one and all of which S. PETER emphatically states the *universality* of CHRIST's work of salvation; it is to turn " every " one of them from his iniquities; " nay, it is to culminate in a time of renewal of all things, as our next citation shall shew beyond any possibility of doubt.

ACTS iii, 21.

"WHOM THE HEAVENS MUST RECEIVE UNTIL THE TIMES OF RESTITUTION OF ALL THINGS, WHICH GOD HATH SPOKEN BY THE MOUTH OF ALL HIS HOLY PROPHETS SINCE THE WORLD BEGAN."

Can the Bible speak more distinctly? Can words be plainer, clearer, more explicit? *All things are to be restored;* and this is said to be the meaning of the work of CHRIST, the meaning of the promise to ABRAHAM, of the Jewish covenant (v. 25, and c. ii, 17), the meaning of the outpoured spirit. This is the language held by all the Prophets since the world began. I repeat, either these words of the Apostle are untrue, or there shall one day be a universal restoration— *all* things made new—*all* men saved.

ACTS iii, 25.
"SAYING UNTO ABRAHAM, IN THEE SHALL ALL THE KINDREDS OF THE EARTH BE BLESSED."

Here is the blessed purpose of GOD, which St. PAUL speaks of as a promise that ABRAHAM should be '*heir of the world*' (*Rom.* iv, 13) ; the purpose by which GOD chooses a people as " first " fruits " of all the earth ; and so implies the salvation of all men.

If in these comments the same ideas recur, that is because in Scripture they too recur ; and I feel it right to press on your attention this very fact of their reiterated mention in the Bible. Let me close this chapter, as I began, by remarking that I have throughout, merely assumed the Bible to mean what it says. I dare not do otherwise, for—to take one instance—I can hardly conceive a greater *insult* offered to CHRIST than to say, that *professing to draw all men unto Himself He really only means to draw some men.*

"WHAT THE NEW TESTAMENT TEACHES."

"Love—hopeth *all* things."—I Cor. xiii, 7.

"I think all the ways lead to our Father," said the little Pilgrim (though she had not known this till now), "and the dear Lord walks about them all. Here you never go astray."—*A Little Pilgrim in the Unseen*, p. 62.

"With me, this final victory (of good over evil), is not a matter of speculation at all, but of absolute faith; and to disbelieve it would be for me *to cease altogether to trust or to worship God*"—Bishop Ewing.

"I have a creed," I replied, "none better and none shorter. It is told in two words, the two first of the Paternoster. And when I say these words I mean them."—O. W. Holmes, *Autocrat of the Breakfast Table*.

CHAPTER VII.

"WHAT THE NEW TESTAMENT TEACHES."

In the last chapter we saw how very numerous are the passages which the writings of *S. Matthew, S. Luke,* and *S. John* contain, clearly asserting the salvation of all men, or implying it by necessary inference. We now, in the present chapter, proceed to consider the many and weighty declarations, to the same effect, furnished by the epistles of *S. Paul, S. Peter*, and that to the *Hebrews.* I may here say, that we shall find in these books the stream of promise still widening —the blessed purpose of Redemption as universal in its effects—indicated with a precision of language, and a variety of illustration, convincing to any fair mind.

As we read these passages of Holy Scripture, our *surprise increases to amazement* at those who, within the Church and without it, do in fact desire us to return to the bondage of mediæval tradition on this subject of future punishment. Nay, that is to *understate* the case, for, even in the darkest middle ages, men would not believe that cruel dogma of endless torment in all its present cruelty. They had not then quite forgotten the teaching of earlier and purer days, and, as has been explained, the belief in Hell was then so completely tempered by the doctrine of Purgatory as to lose more than half its terrors. So that in very deed in asking all men to believe, and clergy and ministers to teach, endless torture in Hell—unrelieved by any terminable punishment beyond the grave—they are not merely reproducing the cruel beliefs of the darkest ages, but they are positively seeking to *aggravate their terrors; to open for us beyond and " beneath the " lowest depth, a lower deep" of horror, unutterable and inconceivable.*

ROMANS iv, 3.

"FOR THE PROMISE THAT HE SHOULD BE THE HEIR OF THE WORLD WAS NOT TO ABRAHAM, OR TO HIS SEED THROUGH THE LAW, ETC."

Here remark how distinct is the assertion—how clear and precise—that in the promise to ABRAHAM is implied a universal blessing. The election by GOD of the Jews really involves *the world's* salvation; for ABRAHAM is " heir of the " world," *i.e.*, receives, as his inheritance, the *whole* world. In a later chapter (ch. ix) I have pursued at more length this all important fact, that the essential idea involved in the Divine election, is by it to convey a blessing to *all*; not to offer, but actually to impart this blessing.

ROMANS v, 15-18

"BUT NOT AS THE OFFENCE, SO ALSO IS THE FREE GIFT. FOR IF THROUGH THE OFFENCE OF ONE MANY BE DEAD, MUCH MORE THE GRACE OF GOD, AND THE GIFT BY GRACE, WHICH IS BY ONE MAN, JESUS CHRIST, HATH ABOUNDED UNTO MANY. THEREFORE AS BY THE OFFENCE OF ONE, JUDGEMENT CAME UPON ALL MEN TO CONDEMNATION; EVEN SO BY THE RIGHTEOUSNESS OF ONE THE FREE GIFT CAME UPON ALL MEN UNTO JUSTIFICATION OF LIFE."

I cannot but earnestly commend a study of these verses, and with them, of the whole drift and argument of the passage. It is, I do not fear to assert, *absolutely irreconcilable* with a partial salvation, It contains a statement as explicit as words can convey it, of this great truth—GOD's remedy is stronger than sin. Wherever, upon whomsoever sin has lighted, there shall GOD's grace, through JESUS CHRIST, come to heal. In the very same sense as "the many" (all men) were made sinners, so the "many" shall have righteousness—not merely offered them—but be made righteous. Less than this cannot satisfy the original text, about the meaning of which there is no question at all. Will the advocates of the popular creed explain how the grace of GOD (v. 15) can be *mightier*, in fact, than the Fall, if there be a Hell ringing to all eternity with the groans of the lost? Will they explain how grace can *much more* abound than the offence—if there be a place of endless torture to punish the offence—if the offence be never taken away?

ROMANS viii, 18-19-21-22 23.

"FOR I RECKON THAT THE SUFFERINGS OF THIS PRESENT TIME ARE NOT WORTHY TO BE COMPARED WITH THE GLORY WHICH SHALL BE REVEALED IN US. FOR THE EARNEST EXPECTATION OF THE CREATURE WAITETH FOR THE MANIFESTATION OF THE SONS OF GOD. BECAUSE THE CREATURE ITSELF ALSO SHALL BE DELIVERED FROM THE BONDAGE OF CORRUPTION INTO THE GLORIOUS LIBERTY OF THE CHILDREN OF GOD. FOR WE KNOW THAT THE WHOLE CREATION GROANETH AND TRAVAILETH IN PAIN TOGETHER UNTIL NOW. * * WAITING FOR THE ADOPTION, TO WIT, THE REDEMPTION OF OUR BODY."

Here is a glorious passage in which the larger hope is not dimly, but explicitly taught—taught with absolute clearness. As to the details of St. PAUL's meaning, men may fairly differ; but his central thought is clear. All created things have been subjected to vanity—to pain and suffering. Yet these are but the travail pains of a new birth; all that suffers shall be delivered from the bondage of corruption. Note how here (alone in the New Testament I think) are the sufferings of the whole creation alluded to, and how emphatic is the assertion that *every created thing—pasa he ktisis*—is awaiting Redemption.

ROMANS viii, 32.

"HE THAT SPARED NOT HIS OWN SON, BUT DELIVERED HIM UP FOR US ALL, HOW SHALL HE NOT WITH HIM ALSO FREELY GIVE US ALL THINGS." *(Ta panta.)*

GOD's gift of HIS SON means giving man *every thing*, *i.e.*, all things—all persons. True, the elect are primarily here referred to, but the elect are only the representatives of all (see the quotations following). And if the elect are given all things, surely they are given the eternal salvation of all their brethren. If this were not so, how could they have all things? (*I Cor.* iii, 21-23).

ROMANS xi, 15-16.

"FOR IF THE CASTING AWAY OF THEM BE THE RECONCILING OF THE WORLD, WHAT SHALL THE RECEIVING OF THEM BE, BUT LIFE FROM THE DEAD ? FOR IF THE FIRST FRUIT BE HOLY, THE LUMP IS ALSO HOLY."

Here are neglected truths plainly stated. The calling of the Jews is linked in GOD's plan with the world's salvation (v. 12). They are HIS people, in the truly divine sense, that by them the world's salvation may be worked out. They, as 'first fruits,' represent and pledge the world—this is the true election and this only—and JESUS CHRIST has, by HIS Cross, made of Jew and Gentile " one new man "—suggestive words (*Eph.* ii, 15). ABRAHAM is thus made, in Scripture phrase, the " heir of the world." But it is precisely this breadth of the Divine purpose that the Bible is so anxious to enforce, and the popular creed so anxious to deny.

ROMANS xi, 26.
"AND SO ALL ISRAEL SHALL BE SAVED."

Not one soul therefore lost finally; not a Dives—not a Judas—if *all* shall be saved. And Israel is but a type of all mankind. Israel is the election--but GOD'S election means, that in Israel " all the families of the earth shall be " blessed."

ROMANS xi, 29.
"FOR THE GIFTS AND CALLING OF GOD ARE WITHOUT REPENTANCE."

That is, what GOD gives, HE gives effectually. When HE calls, men *must hear*—a fact of the deepest significance, and yet so generally forgotten, in considering the plan of salvation. HE intends HIS salvation to be effectually offered to all men through JESUS CHRIST.

ROMANS xl, 32.
"FOR GOD HATH CONCLUDED THEM ALL IN UNBELIEF, THAT HE MIGHT HAVE MERCY UPON ALL."

Words that surely need no comment. *All* in

unbelief—in order to the salvation of *all*. Where then is any room for a partial salvation?

ROMANS xi, 36.

"FOR OF HIM, AND THROUGH HIM, AND TO HIM, ARE ALL THINGS."

Compare this with the promise of that time, when GOD shall be All in All; and look at the context—these words are St. PAUL's burst of joy as he discerns a glorious future, a time when all things, without exception, shall be summed up in GOD. Here it is worth while to sum up clearly a few of the conclusions of this wonderful chapter, viz. :—

a. GOD's rejection of Israel is apparent only, for HIS calling is indefeasible, and therefore

b. *All* Israel shall be saved—without exception.

c. Israel, *i.e.* the elect, is so closely linked with the world, that their very rejection means the world's salvation—in GOD's mysterious plan.

d. So close is this tie between the elect and the world, that a further promise follows, that Israel's restoration shall be to the world " life "*from the dead*"—v.15—in itself a very suggestive phrase as to GOD's way of giving life—see ch. ix.

ROMANS xiv, 9-11-12.

"FOR TO THIS END CHRIST BOTH DIED, AND ROSE, AND REVIVED, THAT HE MIGHT BE LORD BOTH OF THE DEAD AND LIVING. FOR IT IS WRITTEN, AS I LIVE, SAITH THE LORD, EVERY KNEE SHALL BOW TO ME, AND EVERY TONGUE SHALL CONFESS TO GOD. SO THEN EVERY ONE OF US SHALL GIVE ACCOUNT OF HIMSELF TO GOD."

Death does not affect CHRIST'S power over all —or HIS purpose to bring all into harmony with HIMSELF—perhaps as hinted here by judgement (see ch. 9). To HIM is assigned an empire—to which death can set no limit—to which, emphatically there is no end.

I CORINTHIANS xv, 22.

"FOR AS IN ADAM ALL DIE, EVEN SO IN CHRIST SHALL ALL BE MADE ALIVE.

Few passages are more exultant than this, in which St. PAUL tells how complete, how universal, the victory of CHRIST shall be. He starts in the text by asserting a great, but forgotten, principle—the *oneness* of mankind—(on which see above p. 57). And remember, as ADAM actually brought death, spiritually, to all, so the second ADAM actually brings life, spiritually, to all. No offer of life can for a moment satisfy the plain language of the text. Nothing less than life really—spiritually imparted to all by the second ADAM—can fairly express St. PAUL'S meaning. In plain words, St. PAUL is here distinctly teaching the salvation of all men.

I CORINTHIANS xv, 25 28.

"FOR HE MUST REIGN, TILL HE HATH PUT ALL ENEMIES UNDER HIS FEET. * * THAT GOD MAY BE ALL IN ALL."

A dominion absolutely endless--boundless, is here claimed for CHRIST--all enemies, and all the power of the enemy, yield in submission to HIM. Where is a prospect so glorious as this? It points to the End (v. 24); when the many ages of this dispensation shall have passed, and CHRIST shall finally have triumphed; when the last straying sheep shall have been found; when the last enemy shall have been overcome; then CHRIST shall lay down the kingdom, and God be "All "and in All." There is here, *at the End*, no place for sin—no trace of evil—no Hell—for is not GOD *All and in All?*

I CORINTHIANS xv, 55-57.

"O DEATH, WHERE IS THY STING ? O DEATH, WHERE IS THY VICTORY ?" *(The true reading.)*

Fitly do these words close this chapter, with a prospect of *universal* victory over every opposing power. I ask my readers quietly to think over the whole drift of this chapter; to mark the Apostle's increasing rapture, as his argument expands, and as the prospect opens before him of a universe yet to be, from which every form of evil is banished. Let them consider these two thoughts, ever present to the Apostle's mind here: the *oneness* of mankind in CHRIST, and the *certainty* and *universality* of CHRIST's victory; let them, with S. PAUL, look on in thought to the End, when GOD shall be All in All; then let them say if the salvation of all men be not taught in Holy Scripture.

II CORINTHIANS v, 14.

"FOR THE LOVE OF CHRIST CONSTRAINETH US; BECAUSE WE THUS JUDGE, THAT IF ONE DIED FOR ALL THEN ALL DIED."

This is the true rendering: so close is the union between CHRIST and mankind, (not some men) that in the death of CHRIST *all men died*. All actually shared that death, here is again the great truth of the Solidarity of men; the Atonement is actual, not potential for every human being: actual and indefeasible, not for the elect, but for all: * and pursuing this train of thought S. PAUL tells how :—

II CORINTHIANS v, 19.

"GOD WAS IN CHRIST RECONCILING THE WORLD UNTO HIMSELF."

Here is once more stated the extent of CHRIST's work, it is the world reconciled, and no less than the world. The question is, by what right do we limit its efficacy, when GOD assures us that HIS gifts and calling are without repentance, and

---

* St. PAUL's words, in v. 13, would almost seem to imply that the vastness and universality of the Gospel plan had carried him at times out of himself, as he endeavoured to realise its magnificence.

His purpose immutable? Is God in earnest? does He *mean what He says?* I speak with reverence. This is a question that must surely often rise unbidden, as we read these statements of the Bible, and compare them with the popular creed, which so often turns "all" into "some," when salvation is promised to "all," and turns the "world," when that is said to be saved, into a mere fraction of men.

GALATIANS iii, 8.
"IN THEE SHALL ALL NATIONS BE BLESSED."

The force of texts like this lies in the fact, that they shew the true meaning of God's election, and that they are links in that great chain of promise—of blessing to *all* men—which St. Peter assures us God spake by the mouth of all His holy Prophets, and which he declares to mean the restitution of all things.

EPHESIANS i, 10.
"THAT IN THE DISPENSATION OF THE FULNESS OF THE TIMES, HE MIGHT GATHER TOGETHER IN ONE ALL THINGS IN CHRIST, BOTH WHICH ARE IN HEAVEN AND WHICH ARE ON EARTH; EVEN IN HIM."

Could the writer of these words have really believed—could he have possibly believed—in a Hell swallowing up its myriads of victims? What can convey the idea of a future, in which all things—all the universe—shall be brought to Christ, if this passage does not convey it? But if the universe, and its contents, are summed up in CHRIST, where is any possibility of an endless Hell? How shall it exist—when all shall exist in CHRIST? Remark the contrast, for it is significant. All shall be in CHRIST, says St. PAUL, many—very many—shall be in Hell for ever, says the popular creed. So vast, the Apostle states, is the hope of HIS calling (v. 18)—such the exceeding greatness of HIS power. By this CHRIST was raised and set in Heavenly places, far above all dominion, and as our next quotation shall shew :—

EPHESIANS i, 22.
"GOD HATH PUT ALL THINGS UNDER HIS FEET."

Yes, to JESUS CHRIST *all* are to be brought—all things are to bend to HIM. Now can you—forgive my repeating the question—find place for Hell torments in a universe in which *everything* is to be summed up in JESUS CHRIST, in which *every* knee is to bend to HIM, and to HIM *every* tongue to confess? Do answer this fairly? With our thoughts, as were St. PAUL'S, full of this all-glorious consummation, let us just notice briefly, as we pass, two verses a little further on in the epistle, which are full of the same hope indirectly.

EPHESIANS iii, 8.
"THE UNSEARCHABLE RICHES OF CHRIST."

Not unsearchable surely, if limited by the brief

span of human life in their power to save the lost; not unsearchable, if the Redemption He wrought end in even a partial failure, nay, in failure in even a single case.

EPHESIANS iii, 20.
"To Him that is able to do exceeding abundantly above all that we ask or think."

How shall we, with all these reiterated texts fresh in our minds, in any wise narrow that which CHRIST shall do for sinners? How shall we, or can we, rightly place *any limit, or bound, or end* to His salvation and His empire over men? Do not tell me, with such words of Holy Scripture in our memories, that we err if we think nobly of the future of man: our error is surely this, that we do not think nobly enough, even in our most hopeful moments!

EPHESIANS iv, 10.
"He ascended up far above all heavens, that He might fill all things."

But if CHRIST is to fill all things —the universe —how can evil subsist eternally?

COLOSSIANS i, 15-19-20.
"Who is the image of the invisible God, the first-born of every creature: For it pleased the Father that in Him should all fullness dwell; And, having made peace through the blood of His cross, by Him

> TO RECONCILE ALL THINGS UNTO HIMSELF; BY
> HIM, I SAY, WHETHER THEY BE THINGS* IN
> EARTH, OR THINGS IN HEAVEN."

I ask you carefully to read and consider this passage, and say, if it does not contain a clear statement that CHRIST is the "first-born" of all creation, and thus sums up in HIMSELF all, not the elect or the holy, but mankind (see pages 57-59), whose *solidarity is thus affirmed*? I ask you further, in all calmness to weigh the words in which S. PAUL traces this prerogative of JESUS CHRIST through creation up to redemption; to take in their simple grandeur the words, which tell how HE on and by the Cross reconciled all things unto HIMSELF, whether on earth or in Heaven. I ask you finally what these words can mean if they do not mean a *certain* restitution of *all* things? Can the Apostle mean less than this?

PHILIPPIANS ii, 10-11.

> "THAT AT THE NAME OF JESUS EVERY KNEE
> SHOULD BOW, OF THINGS IN HEAVEN, AND
> THINGS IN EARTH, AND THINGS UNDER THE
> EARTH; AND THAT EVERY TONGUE SHOULD
> CONFESS THAT JESUS CHRIST IS LORD, TO THE
> GLORY OF GOD THE FATHER."

This is S. PAUL's statement of the great vision of the *Apocalypse* (*Rev.* v. 13), in which every

---

* Observe here, as elsewhere, S. PAUL seems to provide against a possible or a probable doubt as to the extent of this reconciliation by repeating his assertion and emphasising it.

created thing in heaven and on earth and under the earth unites to sing—Blessing, etc., to GOD most high. Could a picture more universal be painted—*every* knee, in heaven, on earth, under the earth? But if every created thing swells the chorus, there can be none left shut up in endless pain; there can be no soul finally lost.

PHILIPPIANS iii, 21.
"ABLE EVEN TO SUBDUE ALL THINGS UNTO HIMSELF."

In what sense this subjugation of all things to CHRIST is to be understood (if indeed any doubt could exist), is clear from such passages as ch. ii, 9-11 of this epistle. It is not the driving into Hell of blaspheming myriads; it is every knee bent in JESUS' name; and every tongue confessing HIM.

I. TIMOTHY ii, 3-4.
"GOD OUR SAVIOUR, WHO WILL HAVE ALL MEN TO BE SAVED."

One must be careful not to confound the divine will and that of man. GOD'S will must be effectual, because with HIM to will and to do are the same. And note the context of this passage: prayer, intercessions, and giving of thanks are to be made for *all* men (v. 1), because this pleases GOD who wills the salvation of *all*: "for there is one GOD and one Mediator, JESUS "CHRIST, who gave HIMSELF as a ransom for *all*."

I TIMOTHY iv, 10.

"THE LIVING GOD, WHO IS THE SAVIOUR OF ALL MEN, SPECIALLY OF THOSE THAT BELIEVE."

Any possible obscurity in this passage becomes clear the moment we reflect on GOD's plan by which the elect—those who believe—are first saved, and then become the means, here or in the ages yet to come, of saving all men; as will be more fully explained in a subsequent chapter (ch. ix). Note, the clear statement that GOD is (actually) the Saviour of all men. In saying GOD is the Creator of all men, no one doubts that a universal creation is meant, so in saying GOD is the Saviour of all men, a universal salvation is assuredly meant.

II TIMOTHY i, 10.

"OUR SAVIOUR JESUS CHRIST, WHO HATH ABOLISHED DEATH."

Death is *abolished*, and with death that which it in Scripture implies, sin and evil. For death abolished and Hell maintained for ever are plain contradictions. Again, we may very well ask those who maintain the doctrine of conditional immortality, how death can be abolished, and yet swallow up finally all sinners in a sentence of annihilation—as they teach—(a plain absurdity)?

TITUS ii, 11.

"FOR THE GRACE OF GOD THAT BRINGETH SALVATION HATH APPEARED TO ALL MEN."

Yes, to all men, salvation: this is precisely

the larger hope. But how is " salvation brought " to all men " consistent with the damnation of myriads of men—nay, of any man ?

I PETER iii, 19.

"HE ALSO WENT AND PREACHED UNTO THE SPIRITS IN PRISON."

If we believe these words of the Apostle, they amount to a complete overthrow of the popular view of the state of the sinful dead; for plainly these words do shew a process of redemption as *going on after death*, which the popular creed flatly denies. Remark, too, who they were to whom CHRIST preached: they were not those who had previously no chance of salvation, but they seem to have been those who had sinned against the greatest light known in their day :— They were those who had been disobedient in the days of NOAH. Yet it was to these men that JESUS went with HIS offer of salvation, after their earthly probation was over, after they had been shut up 'in prison.' And let us remember that this is not inserted in the New Testament idly : it is designed to teach us; and what it is designed to teach may surely best be expressed in, or at least gathered from words which I make no apology for quoting again and again, " JESUS " CHRIST is the same to-day as HE was yesterday, " and for ever the same," *i.e.*, the same behind the veil as before it, the same Saviour of the *dead* as of the living.

I PETER iv, 6.

"FOR THIS CAUSE WAS THE GOSPEL PREACHED ALSO TO THEM THAT ARE DEAD, THAT THEY MIGHT BE JUDGED ACCORDING TO MEN IN THE FLESH, BUT LIVE ACCORDING TO GOD IN THE SPIRIT."

Words, these, surely full of hope! Notice again here the connection between judgement and salvation (see v. 5). St. PETER in this reference to the preaching of the gospel to the *dead*, must have--as just remarked--intended a lesson to the Christians of his day, and of our day ; must have meant a hint as to what GOD's plan of mercy in the full extent is, else the reference could hardly have been made. Here we see sinners *dead* and *judged* and yet, in very deed, *evangelised—saved—alive* to GOD in the spirit. How truly scriptural the larger hope is! How truly unscriptural the limiting of GOD's mercy and CHRIST's ministry of salvation, by the fact of death, as the popular creed teaches.

II PETER iii, 9.

"THE LORD IS NOT SLACK CONCERNING HIS PROMISE, AS SOME MEN COUNT SLACKNESS ; BUT IS LONG-SUFFERING TO US-WARD, NOT WILLING THAT ANY SHOULD PERISH, BUT THAT ALL SHOULD COME TO REPENTANCE."

If, then, any do perish, GOD's will and design must have been successfully resisted ; a thing absurd, for both are immutable.

HEBREWS ii, 8-9.
"THOU HAST PUT ALL THINGS IN SUBJECTION
UNDER HIS FEET, ETC."

This is to be compared with that very large class of passages which speak so clearly of CHRIST'S kingdom as destined to extend over all things (*e.g.*, *Eph.* iv, 10; i, 10; *Phil.* iii, 9-11; *Rev.* v, 13); as an empire absolutely universal, destined to be co-extensive with all creation. I do not see how the true force of these texts can be found, except in the fact of CHRIST'S being destined to reign in the hearts of all men one day. It is of CHRIST'S *redemption* these passages all speak, not of HIS rule apart from that; and so here verse 9 ends thus: "That HE by the "grace of GOD should taste death for every man." But this is clearly brought out as the true meaning when we read as follows—in the same connection and as a sequel:—

HEBREWS ii, 14.
"THAT THROUGH DEATH HE MIGHT DESTROY
HIM THAT HAD THE POWER OF DEATH, THAT IS,
THE DEVIL."

But the destruction of the DEVIL is inconsistent with the continuance of death and evil (if words are to have any meaning at all).

HEBREWS vi, 17.
"THE IMMUTABILITY OF HIS COUNSEL."

Yes, on this we build! Would you know

what His counsel is? turn to *II Peter* iii, 9:
"Not willing that any should perish, but (willing)
"that all should come to salvation." The word
translated, 'willing,' is the same as the 'counsel'
of this passage. And thus, if His will is immutable—a partial salvation becomes impossible.

HEBREWS viii, 10-11.

"FOR THIS IS THE COVENANT THAT I WILL MAKE WITH THE HOUSE OF ISRAEL AFTER THOSE DAYS, SAITH THE LORD; I WILL PUT MY LAWS INTO THEIR MIND, AND WRITE THEM IN THEIR HEARTS: AND I WILL BE TO THEM A GOD, AND THEY SHALL BE TO ME A PEOPLE: AND THEY SHALL NOT TEACH EVERY MAN HIS NEIGHBOUR, AND EVERY MAN HIS BROTHER, SAYING, KNOW THE LORD: FOR ALL SHALL KNOW ME, FROM THE LEAST TO THE GREATEST."

This is spoken of the New Covenant, and is a distinct statement of its true extent. *All, from the least to the greatest*, are to know GOD. Now, can a partial salvation really be said to satisfy these plain words, on any principle of common *honesty* of interpretation, of common *truthfulness*?

HEBREWS ix, 26.

"NOW ONCE IN THE END OF THE WORLD HATH HE APPEARED TO PUT AWAY SIN BY THE SACRIFICE OF HIMSELF."—*Rev. Version*

See how very significant the words are, it is the *destruction* of sin, its annihilation that is said to be the object of the manifestation of JESUS CHRIST. But this annihilation of sin and evil cannot by any fairness of interpretation take place if Hell and its horrors go on for ever. Sin *put away*—all sin abolished—is the promise of the text and the hope of the universalist.

HEBREWS xiii, 8.
"JESUS CHRIST THE SAME YESTERDAY, AND TO-DAY, AND UNTO (THROUGHOUT) THE AGES."— *So in the Original.*

The same throughout 'the ages;' words little heeded, I fear, and yet which contain indeed the very essence of the Gospel—the very sum and substance of the true hope for our race. I rejoice to close with such a passage this long list of texts from Holy Scripture, which one and all testify to the assured hope there is in JESUS CHRIST of the salvation of every child of ADAM. For what is it these words teach? not that CHRIST is now a saviour, and will in future be merely a judge to condemn, but that what HE was on earth that is HE now, and that HE will be through 'the ages' (judging ever, but only a judge that HE may by it be a saviour). "These "words imply that through the ages a saviour is "needed, and will be found as much as to-day "and yesterday."

Indeed I might almost say, that this passage holds the key to the whole mystery of future punishment, and future salvation. It bids us look beyond the present life, to a series of ages yet to come, and there see JESUS CHRIST still working to save ; doubtless by penalty, by sharp discipline, by fiery trial in the case of hardened sinners, but still through 'the ages' the same JESUS, *i.e.*, Saviour, and destined to continue HIS work of salvation till the last wanderer shall have been found.

And here let me say, that this series of passages of Holy Scripture, lengthened as it is, might easily have been still increased. So far from producing every possible passage that teaches the larger hope, I might have easily cited other texts that teach, or imply the same. In proof of this, let me but take two clauses of the Lord's Prayer ; " Our Father," these two words really involve the whole question—they convey all I teach -- are the charter of our humanity—they form a tie never to be broken between man and GOD. " Thy will be done on earth as in Heaven." But how is HIS will done in Heaven? it is *universally* done. Shall it not then be *universally* done on earth too? Does JESUS CHRIST put into our mouths a petition which HE does not design to fulfil, nay, to fulfil in larger measure than we can hope ? Would you have further proof how true it is that I have not exhausted all the passages of the New Testament that teach the larger hope ?—although I prefer to appeal on this point (see p. 4) to the Divine justice—I have but to quote the memorable words, which may fitly wind up the series, " GOD is love " . To this point all HIS attributes converge. Love is the name of that character, which united they form (love eternal, infinite, divine). Can this love, by any possibility, consign to hopeless, endless, agony, its own children? Could this love, by any possibility, have called into being any one creature knowing that unending torture would be its fate? Can infinite love ever cease to love—can love essential ever fail?—let the Apostle reply, " Love *never faileth*." *

A few words of earnest caution must be added here. I trust it has been made plain in these pages, that in teaching universal salvation, I have not for a moment advocated the salvation of sinners while they continue such. Far other is the view maintained here: it is the certain punishment of sin I teach—GOD's judgement upon all sin (a judgement awful it may well be in its duration and in its nature for the hardened offender), but in all cases directed by love and justice to the final extirpation of sin. Nay, I have opposed the popular creed on this very ground (pp. 5 and 34) that it in fact teaches

---

* In the above brief notes I have not attempted an exhaustive comment. It has been my aim to point out the plain natural meaning of the passages cited, in their bearing on the future destiny of man, and to present this meaning in the most simple and straightforward way. Specially have I urged the imperative necessity of truthfulness, of assuming that what the sacred writers say, that they mean, in the ordinary acceptation of their words—that in saying, *e.g.*, 'I make all ' things new,' CHRIST really means all things and not some things; that in saying ' GOD is the Saviour of all men,' the Apostle means that GOD really does save all men.

men to make light of sin, and that in two ways: first because it sets forth a scheme of retribution so unjust as to make men believe its penalties will never be inflicted; and next because it in fact asserts that GOD either will not or cannot overcome and destroy evil and sin, but will bear with them to all eternity; will permit them to continue defiling and darkening His universe for ever and ever. Let me then say with all due emphasis, that not one word has been written in these pages tending to represent GOD as a merely good natured Being—all-indulgent to the sinner —who regards as a light matter the violation of His holy law. Such shallow theology, GOD forbid that I should teach. It is, I fully admit, in the light of Calvary that we are bound to see the true guilt of sin. But let us beware lest, as we stand in thought at the foot of the Cross, we dishonour the Atonement by limiting its power to save—by teaching men that it does *in fact* fail to save countless myriads—that CHRIST is after all not the victor but the vanquished! Nay, let us beware lest in words professing to honour CHRIST, we in fact make *Him a liar*; for HE has never said, 'I, if I be lifted up, will draw some 'men,' or even 'most men,' but 'I will draw *all* 'men unto me.'

"WHAT THE NEW TESTAMENT TEACHES."

"The word Hell, the sacred writers *never* use, in the sense which "is generally given to it."—Dr. ERNEST PETAVEL—*The Struggle for Eternal Life.*

"The first class of Scriptures we have to examine are those in "which the words 'Hell' and 'damnation' occur, for it is on these "passages mainly that the popular misconception is based * * * "No doubt many of you will be surprised * * * to hear that "*neither of these words is to be found in any part of the New Testament,* "*or indeed in any part of the whole Bible;* nor any word which at all "answers to the conception which they quicken in our minds. 'Not "to be found in the New Testament,' you say, 'why, I can shew "you a dozen or a score of places in which these words are to be "found.' But are you quite sure that it is the New Testament in "which you find them? It is a version, a translation, of the New "Testament of course; but does it necessarily follow that the "translation is an accurate one? I am sorry to say that in so far "as it uses the words 'Hell' and 'damnation' it is demonstrably an "inaccurate and misleading one."—S. COX, D.D., *Salvator Mundi,* page 39.

"Dr. CLAPP proceeds to give an account of his studies:—Carefully "reading through the Old Testament in Hebrew, he was unable to "find the doctrine he sought (that of endless punishment), or even "to find in the Hebrew a word at all corresponding to 'Hell' as a "place of future punishment. * * * Confessing that he could "not find in the Hebrew Old Testament the text he sought, he still "turned with perfect confidence to the New; but after a study of "eight years was compelled by his conscience to admit that he could "*not find a single text in the Greek Testament which, when fairly* "*interpreted, affirms the endless misery of any human soul.*"—*Theology of the Bible*—Chancellor HALSTED.

"Ideo Dives ille in Evangelio, * * * pœnalibus torquetur "ærumnis, *ut citius possit evadere.*"—S. AMBROSE, in *Ps.* cxviii, 1.

CHAPTER VIII.

"*WHAT THE NEW TESTAMENT TEACHES.*"

In the preceding chapters we have examined the various passages of the New Testament which teach, or imply clearly, the larger hope for all men. In the present chapter I purpose considering the chief texts alleged in favour of the received doctrine; and I hope to shew, that while undoubtedly the penalties threatened against sinners are sharp and terrible, still they are not *endless*. I believe that *no one passage* can be found any where in the Bible that so teaches, when fairly translated and understood. I must ask you, before we proceed to our examination of these passages, to bear in mind the following considerations:—

1. God's threats do not stand on the same footing as His promises; for the latter contain a distinct engagement with those who fulfil the conditions, while His threats differ in containing no such engagement, because no one is aggrieved

although they should not be maintained.

2. A fact of the *deepest significance* is this; that although many terms and phrases existed, by which the idea of unendingness might have been conveyed, yet none of these is applied by our LORD and HIS Apostles to the future punishment of the impenitent. The intent to threaten and to warn the ungodly is no doubt quite clear, but the precise nature and duration of the penalties threatened is *very indefinitely* stated, and *nowhere stated to be unending*.

3. Again, while the texts already quoted in favour of the salvation of all men, use language clear and explicit, and are a fair rendering of the original in all cases, it is not so in the case of the passages usually alleged to prove endless torment. In all cases where they seem to the English reader so to teach, they are either mistranslated or misinterpreted, or both.

4. As instances of wholly incorrect rendering in our version, let me take the words 'Hell' and 'damnation,' * (the terms 'everlasting,' 'eternal,' and 'for ever and ever,' also complete mistranslations, will be elsewhere fully discussed). 'Hell' is really, in our Bibles, the rendering of three

---

* I may again remind my readers how inaccurate is the assumption, all but universally made, that these terms *are in the Bible*. They are merely in a certain human and fallible translation of the Bible, a totally different thing.

widely differing Greek words, viz., "Gehenna," "Hades," and "Tartarus," a fact in itself a sufficient comment on the *accuracy* of our translation. "*Gehenna*" occurs eleven times in the New Testament as used by our LORD, and once by St. JAMES. In the original Greek it is taken almost unchanged from the Hebrew (*Ge-hinnom*, *i.e.*, valley of Hinnom), an example which our translators surely ought to have followed and rendered *Gehenna*, as it is, by *Gehenna*. This valley lay outside Jerusalem: once a pleasant vale and later a scene of Moloch worship, it had sunk into a common cesspit at last. Into it were flung offal, the carcasses of animals, and it would seem, of criminals, and in it were kept fires ever burning (for *purification* be it remembered), while the worms were for ever preying on the decaying matter. The so called undying worm and flame, of which so much has been made (i) were purely temporal and finite (ii), preyed only on the dead body (iii) and were one and all purifactory: three particulars essential to the due understanding of the passages on which the dogma of endless torments has been so unfairly based. *Hades* is a purely classical term, denoting merely the state or place of disembodied spirits after death. Our Revisers have, by a tardy justice, struck Hell as its translation, out of their version. It occurs in the Gospels and Epistles five times, twice in the Acts, and four times in the Revelations. Its true meaning is hardly now a subject of dispute by any one: it denotes that intermediate state, or place, which succeeds death ; a state, which in our recoil from Romish error, we have almost ceased to recognise at all. *Tartarus* occurs once only (in the verbal form) in the New Testament, in *II Peter* ii, 4. It also is a classical term, used there most often, although not always, for the place of future punishment of the wicked. Here St. PETER applies it not to human beings, but to the lost angels, and in their case it denotes *no final place of torment*, but a prison in which they are kept *awaiting* their final judgement, so to render it by the term Hell is simply preposterous.

'Damnation,' 'damned,' both of these terms represent merely two Greek words (and their derivatives), *krino* and *katakrino*, *i.e.*, to judge and to condemn. Our Revisers have felt how unwarrantable the former translation was, for which there is indeed this excuse, that probably, when the authorised version was made, the meaning of the word 'damn' was far milder than it has since become (as was certainly the case with the term 'Hell'). To import into these words the idea of endless torment is to err against all fairness and all reason, for they simply mean to 'judge,' and at most, to 'condemn.' Of endless condemnation there is no thought in the original, in any case where these words occur. [In one passage, *II Peter* ii, 3, the word 'damna-'tion' represents a different Greek word, '*apoleia*,' and is rightly rendered by our Revisers as 'destruction,' in that place.]

Most significant is it that when we look at the original of the New Testament, the whole idea of endless punishment, that we associate with these words, ' Hell ' and ' damnation,' wholly disappears. The horrors of unending agony, which these terms yet conjure up for so many, vanish when we come to know that by 'damnation ' is simply meant ' judgement,' or at most ' condemnation,' as our Revisers now most fully admit in their version of the New Testament, and by ' Hell' is only meant, either the place of disembodied souls—*Hades*—(as our Revisers now render it)—or the Jewish *Gehenna* (see margin of revised version), a place of temporary punishment, where the worms fed continually it is true, and the fire for ever burned ; but in both cases purifying and causing no pain (for the bodies were those of the dead), and where both 'undying' worm, and ' unquenchable ' fire, have long since, in their literal sense, passed away. True it is, most true, that while no unending torment is threatened by our LORD, yet HIS words do convey most weighty and most solemn warning to the sinner—warning that I am persuaded gains in real weight and solemnity when its true import is discerned—because the conscience recognises its justice.

Lastly, let me repeat that I accept heartily and emphatically—in their true natural sense—every warning, however terrible, and every penalty threatened against sinners in GOD's word ; but that true natural sense is not, as I hope to shew, in any one case that of endless torment. My quarrel with the advocates of the popular view (as far as the Scripture is concerned) is that, while assigning to one class of texts a meaning, which they cannot fairly bear, they at the same time wholly put out of view—blot out from the Bible in fact—a very large and weighty class of passages, furnished by the New Testament, in favour of universal salvation. Thus, as so often happens when men persist in seeing only one side, they fail to apprehend the true meaning even of that one side, which they present to us as though it were the whole.

S. MATTHEW iii, 12.

"HE SHALL BURN UP THE CHAFF WITH UN-QUENCHABLE FIRE."

(a) The word 'unquenchable' is hardly a fair rendering of the original—which certainly does not convey the idea of a fire that never can be quenched—but of a fire which cannot be checked or quenched in doing its work. In HOMER, where this word first occurs, it is "applied to "the fire which for a few hours rages in the "Grecian fleet—to the gleam of HECTOR's helmit "—to glory—to laughter and to shouting." In the same popular way, *without a thought of endless duration*, it is found in ecclesiastical writers.

WHAT THE NEW TESTAMENT TEACHES. 149

"Eusebius says of two martyrs, that they were "consumed with 'unquenchable' fire; and again "of other two, that they were destroyed by 'un-"quenchable' fire."—Farrar—*Mercy and Judgement*, p. 406.

(b) If the context be examined it will, I think, appear that the reference is to a present, and then impending, judgement—a present work of Christ, and not a future punishment.

(c) And next, the passage shews, that *all* are to share the fiery baptism of Christ, the baptism of fire that purifies and refines. So Scripture teaches, "Every one shall be salted with fire." — S. *Mat.* ix, 49. Doubtless all that is worthless shall be burned up; but the very purpose of this fire is purification, not torture. See chapter ix, section on 'fire.'

S. MATTHEW v, 22.

"Whosoever shall say thou fool shall be in danger of Hell-fire."

I am not afraid to assert that the popular interpretation is not unfounded alone, but reduces the words of Christ to an absurdity here. "It is incredible that to call a man a fool should "be so much a worse crime than to call him "Raca, that, whereas for the one offence, men "are to be brought before a court of justice, for "the other they are to be damned to an everlast-"ing torment." Need I say further here that the Hell-fire of this passage is the fire of 'Gehenna,' the temporary punishment of the criminal. See note on *S. Mark* ix, 43.

S. MATTHEW xxiii, 33.

"HOW SHALL YE ESCAPE THE DAMNATION OF HELL?"

Not one syllable is needed by way of comment here, but to replace a misleading translation by the true rendering—" How shall ye escape the "judgement of *Gehenna*"—the Jewish punishment awarded to criminals.

MATTHEW v, 29-30, AND xviii, 8-9.

"AND IF THY RIGHT EYE OFFEND THEE PLUCK IT OUT AND CAST IT FROM THEE, FOR IT IS PROFITABLE FOR THEE THAT ONE OF THY MEMBERS SHOULD PERISH, AND NOT THAT THY WHOLE BODY SHOULD BE CAST INTO HELL, ETC., ETC."

These two passages are so similar that they may be considered together, and may be compared with *St. Mark* ix, 43-50, where a full comment is given. Here it is enough to say that the 'Hell' of the text is merely '*Gehenna*,' and the punishment, that temporary one inflicted on evil doers. 'Hell-fire' is the fire of *Gehenna*, already explained, 'Everlasting fire,' of chapter xviii, 8, is æonian fire. See next chapter, sec. on *aionios*.

S. MATTHEW xxv, 46.

"AND THESE SHALL GO AWAY INTO EVERLASTING PUNISHMENT, BUT THE RIGHTEOUS INTO LIFE ETERNAL."

I think it will be found that this oft quoted text, if fairly translated, requires an interpretation quite distinct from that of the popular theology, and opposed to it.

(a) 'Everlasting' and 'eternal,' merely represent the Greek word *aionios*, and mean of or belonging to an age—æonian. See next chapter.

(b) The word translated punishment is a remarkable one, it means, literally, *pruning*, *i.e.*, corrective punishment, and should be so rendered.

(c) So that which is threatened is *the opposite* of our popular Hell; it is an æonian discipline, a corrective process, proper to the age—or ages.

(d) But it will no doubt be said, that the same word is applied to the happiness of the saved and to the punishment of the lost, and that if it does not mean endless in the latter case then the bliss of the redeemed is thus rendered uncertain. I reply, even were it so, we are not at liberty to mistranslate the original: but further, no greater error can be imagined than this assertion. The facts are simply these:—In this passage all that is asserted is that a certain ' æonian ' penalty, and a certain ' æonian ' reward will respectively be the lot of the wicked and of the righteous; so far both the penalty and the reward stand on the same footing. But this *merely leaves open* the whole question of the precise duration of either, so far as the present passage goes. That the ' æonian ' penalty will terminate, we have the clearest assertion elsewhere in Scripture, as the passages discussed in chapters vi and vii amply prove. That the 'æonian' reward will go on unendingly, follows from the very nature of GOD, and of goodness, and from ample Scriptural proof besides.

(e) There is another important question which arises here—to *what time* are we to refer this judgement scene. These words close a continuous discourse extending over chapters xxiv-v. There seems no break throughout. And remember the question of the disciples, in chapter xxiv, is really not about the end of the 'world,' but of the 'age,' and CHRIST HIMSELF says, v. 34, *All* the things HE is speaking of should be fulfilled before the passing away of the then generation. " To judge by a simple straightforward reading " of these chapters, the scene of the Son of Man " sitting upon the throne of HIS glory, belongs " as properly to the time of the destruction of the " temple, as the fleeing of those in Judea into " the mountains."—Rev. J. LLEWELYN DAVIES.

S. MARK ix, 43-50.

"AND IF THY HAND CAUSE THEE TO STUMBLE, CUT IT OFF: IT IS GOOD FOR THEE TO ENTER INTO LIFE MAIMED, RATHER THAN HAVING THY TWO HANDS TO GO INTO HELL, INTO THE UNQUENCHABLE FIRE. AND IF THY FOOT CAUSE THEE TO STUMBLE, CUT IT OFF: IT IS GOOD FOR THEE TO ENTER INTO LIFE HALT, RATHER THAN HAVING THY TWO FEET TO BE CAST INTO HELL. AND IF THINE EYE CAUSE THEE TO STUMBLE,

WHAT THE NEW TESTAMENT TEACHES. 153

CAST IT OUT: IT IS GOOD FOR THEE TO ENTER INTO THE KINGDOM OF GOD WITH ONE EYE, RATHER THAN HAVING TWO EYES TO BE CAST INTO HELL; WHERE THEIR WORM DIETH NOT, AND THE FIRE IS NOT QUENCHED. FOR EVERY ONE SHALL BE SALTED WITH FIRE."--*Rev. Vers.*

(a) Note, first, that the revised text *omits* v. 44 and 46, which lend in our ordinary version so much weight to the threats here uttered.

(b) Observe next that the whole passage depends on the statement of v. 49--a fact generally overlooked—" *For every one* shall be salted " with fire." These words assign the reason for the whole preceding clauses, and indeed seem plainly enough to shew that the true reference in this passage is to some sacrificial or purifying process, which *every one* must undergo; as in *I Cor.* iii, 13, "the fire shall try every man's " work." If the sacrifice be not made voluntarily —if the eye or the foot be not sacrificed—a sharper sacrifice—a severer penalty will be demanded. In an appendix a fuller discussion of this passage will be found.

(c) The word translated Hell is simply, as already explained, the Jewish Gehenna—the valley of Hinnom—a place of purely *temporary* punishment. To turn this into Hell—with all its terrific mediæval horrors annexed —is to violate every rule of fair translation, nay of truth.

(d) The phrase, "where their worm dieth not

"and the fire is not quenched," is quoted from the Old Testament (specially *Isaiah* lxvi, 24). The reference is to the worm and to the fire that preyed on the dead bodies of malefactors, cast out into Gehenna. In the striking metaphor of the East, these worms, and this fire are said not to die, and not to be quenched ; because the fires were kept constantly burning to drive away pollution, and the worm was always preying on the corpses and offal. The phrase, 'into the fire that 'never shall be quenched,' it will be seen disappears in the Revised Version. The original word is the same already commented on in·the note on *S. Matthew* iii, 12, translated 'unquench-'able,' and proved to have been frequently applied to a fire, not merely temporary but often very brief in its duration.

(e) I have already admitted fully the solemn nature of our LORD's threats, in the case of the ungodly, and I desire as fully to recognise that while Gehenna literally and primarily means the valley of that name, and its temporary penalties, there is often, doubtless, also in our LORD's words, an allusion to that dark province of the underworld where the Jews believed the souls of the sinful were punished. But this punishment was not believed by them to be endless, which is the point at issue. Nay, the penalties of Gehenna in this sense were by many of the Jews believed to be of brief, nay, of very brief duration.

S. MARK iii, 29.

"HE THAT SHALL BLASPHEME AGAINST THE HOLY GHOST HATH NEVER FORGIVENESS, BUT IS IN DANGER OF ETERNAL DAMNATION."

I select this passage as a striking instance of the wholly unsatisfactory grounds on which the popular dogma rests. The words, 'hath never 'forgiveness,' really mean in the original 'hath 'not forgiveness,' *eis ton aiona*, ' for or during the 'age'—a period not defined—and indeed seem to imply that *after* the age forgiveness may be had. The words 'eternal damnation' are clearly wrong. Damnation is in any case merely judgement, but the true reading is 'sin,' and the true translation is 'is guilty of an æonian sin,' *i.e.*, as has been just said, a sin, 'the effect of 'which must cling to the sinner in the future age 'or æon.'

S. MARK xiv, 21.

"GOOD WERE IT FOR THAT MAN (JUDAS) IF HE HAD NOT BEEN BORN."

(a) The words, as has been remarked, easily admit of a different rendering, ' good were 'it for HIM, *i.e.*, CHRIST, if that man, *i.e.*, JUDAS, 'had not been born.' Grammatically this translation is faultless.

(b) When we remember how uncompromising in many cases are the Divine threats, which yet are subsequently wholly modified ; and when on the other hand we remember the clear and repeated promises of *universal* salvation already quoted, we may well hesitate, and more than hesitate, before we put such a sense on the woe pronounced on JUDAS, as to make it plainly contradict all these promises of Scripture.

(c) Remember too the special promise that "*all Israel shall be saved.*" JUDAS was assuredly an Israelite.

(d) Remember further, that even if taken in their extremest sense, the words of JUDAS' doom *wholly fail* to prove that he was condemned to endless suffering. They would be satisfied to the utmost if JUDAS were to have sentence of annihilation passed on him at the Last Great Day: nay, had he at the moment of betrayal died "and never suffered one pang more they "would be to the fullest extent true." *

S. LUKE xvi, 26.

THE PARABLE OF DIVES.

(a) DIVES, like JUDAS, is a son of ABRAHAM, "and *all* Israel shall be saved," says St. PAUL expressly.

---

* Even in early days some believed that JUDAS hurried out of this world to obtain CHRIST's forgiveness beyond the grave. We need not endorse this view, but to me it certainly seems as if the heart of JESUS, and the love of JESUS, would not have refused mercy to HIS betrayer on the least sign of repentance in this or another world.

(b) DIVES was certainly not in Hell, but in Hades (as our Revised Version admits), in the intermediate state before the Day of Judgement, not in a state absolutely fixed.

(c) DIVES is represented as distinctly improved by his chastisment; he has learned to think for others. Can GOD by his discipline *produce this amendment merely to crush it out in a future state of hopeless pain?* Is this credible?

(d) It is not said that the gulf shall continue impassable; what is said is, that it is so (was then so). The case is as if a man were imprisoned for a fixed time, and his friends are sternly told "between him and you is a barrier placed "which cannot be passed." This would be exactly true, though the barrier were to be removed, when the fixed period of punishment ceased.

(e) And even were this not so, who are we to say that the gulf, impassable to man, cannot be passed by CHRIST, by HIM who hath the "*Keys of Death and Hell!*"

(f) Besides, the popular interpretation misses the point. The whole parable is meant, not to teach us how a wicked man will find himself in Hell, but how a self-indulgent life here will lead to sharp future suffering and discipline.

(g) Those inclined to doubt what I have above said may be well referred to the words of the great St. AMBROSE, who, commenting on *Ps.* cviii, says thus, "So then that DIVES in the "gospel, although a sinner, is pressed with penal "agonies that he may *escape the sooner*," thus asserting clearly his belief in DIVES' final salvation.

S. JOHN iii, 36.

"HE THAT BELIEVETH NOT THE SON SHALL NOT SEE LIFE, BUT THE WRATH OF GOD ABIDETH ON HIM."

Here the meaning is clear ; the unbeliever, *continuing such*, shall not see life, but if he cease to be an unbeliever, he may surely obtain peace. If it were not so all would be lost. If the sense put popularly on this passage were true, ' no man ' once an unbeliever could have any hope.'

S. JOHN v, 29.

"THEY THAT HAVE DONE EVIL UNTO THE RESURRECTION OF DAMNATION.

Here it is hardly needful to do more than point to the revised translation, ' the resurrection of *judgement*,' not even condemnation, which would be a different Greek word.

We have now considered, if not all, yet certainly all the strongest passages contained in the New Testament, and supposed to teach the popular creed, except those of the mysterious book of *Revelation*. To this let us now turn. And here, at the outset, I protest against the utter

unfairness of attempting to build any definite
theory of Hell on the imagery of a book of
mysterious visions, and full of highly-toned
Oriental metaphors. Its visions speak the
language not of prose but of poetry, and that the
poetry of an Eastern race, far more imaginative
and highly wrought than that of the West. To
judge these metaphors as though they spoke the
language of theology is worse than unfair, it is
even absurd.

Take an instance : turn to chapter xiv, 9-11.
Terrible as it seems at first sight, it is really
concerned with the times of NERO—who is
certainly the Beast. The worshippers of the
Beast who are to be tormented, are his followers,
and the reference in the torment is simply to the
terrible earthly calamities actually happening to
Rome at that epoch. Who, of whatever school
of thought, is there who does not feel a weight
rolled away, when he perceives that the true
meaning of the highly wrought metaphors of this
passage—as to the worshippers of the Beast
being tormented night and day, in the presence
of the Lamb and the Holy Angels—may be
most fully found in these terrible earthly sufferings which befell Rome, "while the Lamb and
"the Holy Angels are, in human language, repre-
"sented as cognisant of this punishment? The
"smoke which ascends for ever and ever," should
be for 'æons of æons,' ' ages of ages.' This is a
phrase borrowed partly from *Genesis* xix, 28, and

partly from *Isaiah* xxxiv, 9-10, both of which refer to *temporal judgements*, "and may very well, in "the highly figurative language of prophecy, "have such application in the Apocalypse, with- "out the remotest allusion to the state of souls "in the world beyond the grave." Even Mr. ELLIOTT, in his *Horæ Apocalypticæ*, explains this passage of merely temporary judgement. See on this subject, *Mercy and Judgement*, p. 470.

Note too in this connection—as showing the true meaning of the highly wrought metaphors of the East—the deeply impassioned language in which ISAIAH describes the temporal calamities of the land of Idumea (in the passage referred to above), its streams are "to be turned into pitch "—*its dust into brimstone—its land into burning* "*pitch—it shall not be quenched night nor day—its* "*smoke is to go up for ever.*" Now when we know that these metaphors —sounding so awfully—do yet refer to merely temporal judgement—to judgements of a momentary duration, so to speak, we shall the better be able to assign its true meaning to all the figurative and poetical language of this book of *Revelation*.

I therefore must ask you to bear ever in mind how unfair, nay impossible, it is to harden into dogmas the glowing metaphors of Eastern poetry if we desire to reach their true meaning. In fact if such language be taken literally its whole meaning is lost. If, *e.g.*, even in the case of some of our LORD's words, which are less figurative—I take them literally—I pervert their sense. Am I in very deed to *hate* my father and mother because CHRIST says it is necessary so to do : or to pluck out my right eye literally ? Or take a case—well put by Canon FARRAR—to shew how widely the true sense of the figures of Scripture differs from the literal meaning. Egypt is more than once said, in the Bible, to have been an *iron furnace* to the Jews, and yet their condition there was so far removed from being one of torment, that they actually said " it was well with us there," and positively sighed for its enjoyments. In common fairness, therefore, I am forced to maintain that no doctrine of endless pain can be based on figures of Eastern imagery. Having then, already considered the well-known passage in ch. xiv, it will be sufficient if I close this chapter by an examination of another often quoted passage.

REVELATION xxi, 8.

" BUT THE FEARFUL AND UNBELIEVING, AND THE ABOMINABLE, AND MURDERERS * * * AND ALL LIARS, SHALL HAVE THEIR PART IN THE LAKE WHICH BURNETH WITH FIRE AND BRIMSTONE : WHICH IS THE SECOND DEATH."

(a) It will be necessary to consider the entire context of this verse if we desire to understand its purport. It opens with the vision of the great white throne, ch. xx, 14, and we find that after the judgement of that Great Day, so far from death and Hell (Hades) continuing, they are " cast into a lake of fire "—very unlike, nay, contradicting the popular view.

(b) Then comes a declaration that GOD is to dwell with men—not with the saints—but with men as such, and that as a consequence, they shall be *His people, and God shall be with them, and be their God.*

(c) It is distinctly said there shall be *no more death, neither sorrow nor crying nor any more pain.* Is this not a denial of an endless Hell rather than an affirmation of it—nay an emphatic denial of such a doctrine?

(d) Then comes a voice from the throne with a glorious promise, "*Behold I make all things "new,*" not some things. Note, too, this promise is remarkably emphasised, it opens with the word " *Behold* " to draw attention to it : it closes with the command to write it, ' for these ' words are true and faithful.' Was there no reason for this? Is there not thus attention drawn to this as the central point of the whole vision—*all things made new.* But this again is a denial of the popular creed.

(e) In close connection with such promises come the highly figurative threats of the lake of fire. It is perhaps just possible that this may imply, although I do not think so, the destruction of those cast into it ; but it is *wholly impossible to understand it as teaching endless torment* in the face of what has just been promised—no more crying, nor pain, v. 4. Therefore, I cannot but conclude, looking at the repeated promises (see 'c' and 'd') of this very passage, which contrast in their *perfect clearness* with the highly figurative language of its threats,* looking at the true meaning of GOD's judgements and at the whole spirit of Holy Scripture—nay, its express declaration of universal pardon--that what is here taught is some sharp, fiery, discipline—a fire that purifies while it punishes--a fire that is, in GOD's mysterious way, an agent in making all things new.

We thus see that the Apocalyptic visions lend as little support to the dogma of endless torment as do the other Scriptures. That doctrine is not, I am deeply persuaded, to be found in a single passage of GOD's word, if translated accurately and fairly interpreted. And here let me, as I conclude this branch of our subject, before passing on, ask those who honestly believe, that with this dogma of Hell-fire is bound up the sole force able to deter men from sin, to remember that to assert this is to contradict the whole weight of human experience. For in every age experience has shewn decisively, that it is not the magnitude

---

* "How little can we build dogmas on such metaphors as the "Devil being cast with the Beasts (NERO and the Roman world- "powers) and the false Prophet—ch. xx, 10-14 —into the lake of fire "and brimstone * * * into which also are to be cast two "such abstract entities as 'Death' and 'Hades.' At any rate this "lake of fire is on the earth ; and immediately afterwards we read of "that earth being destroyed, and of a new Heaven and a new earth, "in which there is to be no more death or curse."—Canon FARRAR.

of the penalty that deters men from sin or crime, it is the certainty of its infliction. Nay, it must be said on the contrary, that few doctrines have done so much in these days to shake the belief in any real punishment of sin hereafter as that of an endless Hell. For, as I have already briefly attempted to prove (p. 38-9), nobody can be found who, *by his acts*, shews that he in fact believes and accepts so terrible a dogma. From this it follows that, so long as it is taught, the whole subject of future punishment becomes, for the mass of mankind, doubtful, shadowy, and unreal. Thus a tone of secret incredulity is fostered, an incredulity which, beginning at this particular dogma assuredly does not end there, but affects the whole of revealed religion.

It is not merely that those who still teach the popular creed thus furnish the sceptic with the choicest of his weapons, by enlisting the moral forces of our nature on the side of unbelief. They do more than this. They thus, unconsciously I admit, but most effectively, teach men to profess a creed with the lips to which the spirit and the life render no vital allegiance. By this means the whole Gospel of Jesus Christ is lowered and discredited, because if men see a doctrine of this kind maintained in words but in fact denied, (because in practice found to be wholly incredible) they will assuredly apply the lesson, so learned of professed belief and real scepticism, to the whole system of Christian truth.

THE SCRIPTURAL DOCTRINE OF 'THE AGES,' OF 'DEATH,' OF 'JUDGEMENT,' OF 'FIRE,' OF 'ELECTION.'

"Who shall separate us from the love of CHRIST?"—*Rom.* viii, 38.

"The infinite love pursues the soul beyond the grave, and there
"has dealings with it."—Bishop FORBES, on the *Articles.*

"The ende of their wrath and punyshemente intendeth nothynge
"elles but the destruction of vices and savynge of menne: wyth so
"usyinge and ordering them that they cannot chuse but be good,
"and what harm so ever they did before, in the residewe of theyr
"life to make amendes for the same."— Sir T. MORE—*Utopia.*

"Do we want to know what was uppermost in the minds of those
"who formed the word for punishment, the Latin *pœna* or *punio:*—
"The root *pu* in Sanscrit which means to cleanse or purify, tells us
"that the Latin derivative was formed not to express mere striking
"or torture, but cleansing—correcting—delivering from the stain of
"sin."—Professor MAX MULLER.

"JESUS lives; henceforth is Death
But the gate of life immortal."

CHAPTER X.

THE SCRIPTURAL DOCTRINE OF "THE AGES," OF "DEATH," OF "JUDGEMENT," OF "FIRE," OF "ELECTION."

In the last chapter we have considered the proofs, often drawn from certain passages of the New Testament, in favour of the ordinary view of future punishment, and have seen how completely they fail to teach its unending character when fairly translated and fairly understood. In the present chapter I propose to complete our examination of the Scriptural argument by a discussion of the teaching of the Bible as to the various topics referred to in the heading of this chapter, which have a very close relation to the subject of future punishment. To this discussion we now turn.

First, let us in order to ascertain the scriptural doctrine of 'the ages,' consider the true meaning of the words *aion* and *aionios*. These are the originals of the terms rendered by our translators 'eternal,' 'everlasting,' 'for ever and ever:' and on this translation, so misleading, and indeed wholly incorrect, a vast portion of the popular dogma of endless torment is built up. I say without hesitation, misleading and incorrect ; for *aion* means ' an age,' a limited period, whether long or short, though often of indefinite length ; and the adjective *aionios* means ' of the age,' 'age-'long,' ' æonian ' and *never* ' everlasting ' (of its own proper force) : it is true that it may be applied as an epithet to things that are endless, but the idea of endlessness in all such cases comes not from the epithet, but only because it is inherent in the object to which the epithet is applied, as in the case of GOD. Indeed so far from endless duration being implied by the term *aionios*, it sometimes includes hardly any idea of duration at all. Sometimes, as in *St. John*, the æonian life (eternal* life) of which he speaks is a life not measured by its duration, but a life in the unseen—life in GOD.

"The word by itself, whether adjective or sub-"stantive, never means endless."—Canon FARRAR.

---

* It is well to remember that in this book I have, as a rule, used the term ' eternal ' in its popular sense of endless.

"The conception of eternity, in the Semitic "languages, is that of a long duration and series "of ages."— Rev. J. S. BLUNT—*Dict. of Theology.* "'Tis notoriously known," says Bishop RUST, "that the Jews, whether writing in Hebrew or "Greek, do by *olam* (the Hebrew word corres- "ponding to *aion*) and *aion* mean any remarkable "period and duration, whether it be of life, or "dispensation, or polity." "The word *aion* is "never used in Scripture, or any where else, in "the sense of endlessness (vulgarly called eter- "nity), it always meant, both in Scripture and "out, a period of time; else how could it have a "plural—how could you talk of the *æons* and "*æons* of *æons* as the Scripture does."—C. KINGSLEY.

As a further illustration of the meaning of *aion* and *aionios* let me point out that in the Greek version of the Old Testament—in use in our LORD's time—these terms are repeatedly applied to things that have long ceased to exist. Take a few instances out of many. Thus the AARONIC priesthood is said to be 'everlasting,' *Num.* xxv, 13. The land of Canaan is given as an 'everlasting' possession, and 'for ever,' *Gen.* xvii and xiii, 15. In *Deut.* xxiii, 3, 'for ever' is distinctly made an equivalent to 'even to their 'tenth generation.' In *Lam.* v, 19, 'for ever 'and ever' is the equivalent of from 'generation 'to generation.' The inhabitants of Palestine are to be bondsmen 'for ever,' *Lev.* xxv, 46.

In *Num.* xviii, 19, the heave offerings of the holy things are a covenant 'for ever.' CALEB obtains his inheritance ' for ever,' *Josh.* xiv, 9, etc. Another instance from the Old Testament may be found in *Isaiah* xxxii, 14, where we are told 'the forts and towers shall be dens *for ever, until* 'the spirit be poured upon us.' These instances * might without difficulty be increased, but enough has probably been said to prove that it is wholly impossible, and indeed *absurd*, to contend that any idea of endless duration is necessarily implied by either *aion* or *aionios.*

Notwithstanding all this, our translation has steadily adhered to the terms ' eternal ' and ' ever- ' lasting ' as the equivalent of *aionios*; against this we have only to offer the strongest protest, the most earnest remonstrance. Meantime I should like further to ask : if *aionios* does indeed mean ' eternal,' how is it that the substantive *aion* is *in no case* translated by the corresponding noun ' eternity ? ' Why have not our translators done this, which on *their own principles* seems obviously required ? I think I can tell you, it would reduce the word of GOD to an absurdity. Let me give you some instances of the result of translating *aion* by *eternity*. In the first place, you would have over and over again to talk of the

---

* So in *Jude* vii, Sodom and Gomorrah are said to be suffering the vengeance of eternal (æonian) fire, *i.e.*, their temporal overthrow by fire.

'eternities.' We can comprehend what 'eternity' is, but what are the 'eternities?' You cannot have more than one eternity. The Doxology would run thus: "Thine is the kingdom, the "power and the glory, 'unto the eternities.'" Take another instance. In the case of the sin against the Holy Ghost, the translation would then be, "it shall not be forgiven him 'neither "in this eternity nor in that to come.'" Our LORD's words, *St. Matt.* xiii, 39. would then run, "the harvest is the end of (the) eternity," which is to make our LORD talk nonsense.

Again, in *St. Mark* iv, 19, the translation should be, "the cares," not of this world, but "the cares of this eternity choke the word." In *St. Luke* xvi, 8, "The children of this world" should be "the children of this eternity." *Romans* xii, 2, should run thus: "Be not con-"formed to this eternity." In *I Cor.* x, 11, the words "upon whom the ends of the world are "come," should be "the ends of the eternities." Take next *Gal.* i, 4: "That HE might deliver "us from this present evil world," should run thus, "from this present evil eternity." In *II Timothy* iv, 10, the translation should be 'DEMAS hath forsaken me, having loved this 'present eternity.' Take a last example, 'Now 'once at the end of the ages hath HE been mani-'fested' should read, on the popular view, 'at the 'end of the eternities.' Let me state the dilemma clearly. *Aion* either means eternity (endless duration) as its necessary or at least its ordinary significance, or it does not. If it does, why have our Translators *never* so rendered it ? If it does not, what right have they to render the adjective *aionios* by the terms 'eternal' and 'everlasting ?'

There is much more to be said. Besides persisting in a rendering so misleading, our Translators have really done further hurt to those who can only read their English Bible. They have, in fact, wholly obscured, a very important doctrine, that of 'the ages,' This when fully understood throws a flood of light on the whole plan of redemption, and the method of the Divine working, as we shall see. It will be interesting if I give you a few instances to illustrate this fact. You will, I think, see how much force and clearness is gained by restoring to the Bible the true rendering of the words *aion* and *aionios*. I will begin by a well-known passage, *St. Matt.* xxiv, 3. There our version represents the desciples as asking JESUS 'what should be the 'sign of the end of the world.' It should be the end of the 'age,' the close, in fact, of the Jewish age or dispensation, marked by the fall of Jerusalem. In *St. Matt.* xiii, 39-40-49, the true rendering is not the end of the 'world,' but of the 'age,' a change of much significance. So *St. John* xvii, 3, ' This is life 'eternal,' should be ' the life of the ages,' *i.e.*, peculiar to those ages in which the scheme of salvation is being worked out. Or take three passages of the Epistle to the *Hebrews* v, 9 ; ix, 12 ; and xiii, 20, 'eternal 'salvation' should be 'æonian' or of the ages ; 'eternal redemption' is 'redemption of the ages,' the 'eternal covenant' is 'the covenant of the 'ages,' the covenant peculiar to the ages of redemption. In *Ephesians* iii, 11 'the eternal 'purpose' is really the purpose of 'the ages,' *i.e.* developed, worked out in 'the ages.' In the same Epistle, chapter iii, 21, there occurs a suggestive phrase, as usual altogether obscured by our version, 'unto all the generations of the age of 'the ages.' Thus it runs in the original, and it is surely not dealing fairly with GOD's word to wrap up this elaborate statement which gives such prominence to the 'ages' in the mere paraphrase of our version 'throughout all ages.' In *I Cor.* x, 11, 'the ends of the world' are the 'ends of 'the ages. In the same Epistle, chapter ii, 6-7-8 the word *aion* occurs four times translated 'world' it should be 'age' or 'ages' in all cases.

Again in *Hebrews* xi, 3, 'by whom HE made 'the world' should be 'the ages.' In *Hebrews* ix, 26, 'now once in the end of the world hath 'HE appeared' should be 'in the end of the ages.' Again the closing words of St. JUDE present us with a remarkable instance of the use of this word *aion*. It is literally, 'To the only GOD, 'be glory, majesty, dominion and power—before 'every age—and now, and unto all the ages,' *i.e.*, before the ages began, and now, and throughout all the ages yet to come. So in *Rev.* i, 6, we have 'glory and dominion' ascribed unto CHRIST, 'unto the ages of the ages,' in the original. Again in *I Tim.* i, 17, 'the King 'eternal' should be 'the King of the ages;' vi, 17, 'charge them that are rich in this world' should be 'in this age.' *II Peter* ii, 17, 'the 'mist of darkness is reserved for ever' should be 'for the age,' for a period finite but indefinite. A striking phrase closes this Epistle, ch. iii, 18— wholly obscured in our translation—which renders 'to HIM be glory both now and for ever,' instead of, as the original requires, 'unto the day of the 'age,' * see v. 8, which explains the reference. This list I might without difficulty have increased, but enough has been said to shew the prominence given in Scripture to the doctrine of 'the ages.' For who can fail to see, in these repeated instances from Holy Scripture, at least some definite purpose in the use of these peculiar terms; or who can refrain from the deepest regret that our Translators should have so steadily refused to acknowledge this plain fact.

Let me now try to state briefly and clearly what the doctrine of 'the ages' is. I borrow the words of Mr. JUKES:—"It will, I think, be found "that the adjective *œonian* whether applied

---

* Take as an instance the hard measure dealt by our revised version to this word *aion*; you will find in a very short compass—the epistle of St. PAUL to the Ephesians—that they employ—to translate it— *four different* English words or phrases (in ch. i, 21, ch. ii, 2, ch. ii, 7, and ch. iii, 11).

"to 'life,' 'punishment,' 'covenant,' 'times,' or
"even GOD HIMSELF, is always connected with
"remedial labour, and with the idea of ages or
"periods, in which GOD is working to meet and
"correct some awful fall." There is present in
the word in fact a certain spiritual or ethical
force, and a reference to 'the ages' in which a
redeeming process is going on. It is the more
needful to insist on this, because in our recoil
from the Roman Catholic teaching about purgatory, masses for the dead, etc., we have gone
too far into the opposite extreme, we have from
our childhood been trained to limit all GOD's
possible dealings with us, to the narrow span of
our brief earthly existence. But surely this is
to shut our eyes to the truer and higher teaching
of the gospel. What does GOD mean by the
repeated reference to these 'ages,' when HE
speaks in the New Testament of HIS redeeming
plan? On the popular view these passages go
for nothing. Is this fair or reasonable? But
by accepting what they plainly teach, we are
enabled to harmonise GOD's threatenings with
HIS clearly expressed purpose to save all men
finally.

Therefore, we who teach the larger hope feel
constrained to believe, that in these 'ages' is
indicated the true scope of redemption, as a vast
plan, the accomplishment of which is spread over
many periods or stages, of which our present life
forms but one, and it may be, a very brief part.

Through these 'ages' it seems clearly taught in Scripture that CHRIST'S work is to go on, for 'CHRIST *is the same* to-day, and yesterday, and 'unto the ages,' *Heb.* xiii, 8 ; and HE assures us that 'HE is alive unto the ages, and has the 'keys of death and of Hades,' *Rev.* i, 18 (the true rendering), words significant in this connection. This, then, on the plain warrant of Scripture (although our translation completely obscures the fact), we believe to be the 'purpose 'of the ages,' *Eph.* iii, 11. We believe that not in this brief life only, but through future ages, CHRIST'S work shall go on till, as we hope from HIS own teaching, the last straying sheep shall have been found by the Good Shepherd. Nay, we are permitted in Holy Scripture a momentary glance beyond that limit—in these all-glorious words :—' Then,' at the expiry it would seem of these ages,* 'cometh the *end*,' when every enemy vanquished, 'CHRIST shall 'have delivered up the kingdom unto GOD, and 'GOD shall be All in All.'—*I Cor.* xv, 24.

Another class of texts, to which I ask your attention, are those which speak of 'death' and 'destruction' as the portion of the ungodly. I have tried to shew how, when we examine the

---

* It is worth while reminding my readers that our revised version has very frequently admitted the correct rendering of *aion* as *age* into the margin. Let us hope that in the final revision, which one day must be undertaken, this rendering will appear in the text.

original and compare text with text, we see that
not an endless hopeless doom is taught, in the
passages most often quoted to prove the popular
creed, but rather a discipline of the 'ages,'
remedial however sharp, and finite however
lengthened it may be. Turning now to the texts,
sufficiently numerous and clear, that denounce
'death' as the sinner's portion ; I may well ask,
what then ? is hope thus finally excluded ? what
is death ?

There are two answers commonly given.
First comes that of the popular creed which says,
death in the case of sinners means *living for ever*
in pain and torment ; so that I am actually required to believe that *death means life protracted
for ever in pain*, and that destruction means
preservation in eternal anguish ! The recoil
from such incredible teaching has produced the
second view of ' death ' as meaning ' annihilation,'
now maintained by those who teach the doctrine
of ' conditional immorality.'—See pp. 11-3.

In answer to this strange and novel teaching,
I would ask, in the words of an author already
quoted, " Are any of the varied deaths which
" Scripture speaks of as incident to man, his non-
" existence or annihilation ? Take as examples
" the deaths referred to by St. PAUL, in the sixth,
" seventh and eighth chapters of the Epistle to
" the *Romans*. We read (ch. vii, 7) ' He that is
" dead is free from sin.' Is this ' death ' which

"is freedom from sin, non-existence or annihila-
"tion? Again, when the Apostle says (ch. vii,
"9) 'I was alive without the law once, but when
"the commandment came, sin revived, and I
"died.' Was this 'death,' wrought in him by
"the law, annihilation? Again, when he says
"(ch. viii, 6), 'To be carnally minded is death,'
"is this death non-existence or annihilation?
"And again, when he says, (ch. viii, 38) 'Neither
"death nor life shall separate us,' is the 'death'
"here refered to annihilation? When ADAM
"died on the day he sinned (*Gen.* ii, 17), was
"this annihilation? when his body died, and
"turned to dust (*Gen.* v, 5), was this annihila-
"tion? Is our 'death in trespasses and sins'
"(*Eph.* ii, 1-2) annihilation? Is our 'death to
"sin' (*Rom.* vi, 11), annihilation. * * * Do
"not these and similar uses of the word prove
"beyond all question, that whatever else these
"deaths may be, not one of them is non-existence
"or annihilation?"

But if death be neither living for ever in pain,
nor annihilation, what then is it? Death is
bodily dissolution; it is for man 'a separation
'from some given form of life which he has lived
'in;' it is the way out of one state of being into
another. Thus understood, how should death
shut out hope? Nor is it really opposed to life,
in fact it is a pathway to life; nay, the very condition of life in many cases. 'Except a corn of
'wheat fall into the ground and die, it abideth

'alone, but *if it die* it bringeth forth much fruit.— *St. John* xii, 24.* Is there not here a great truth hinted at of universal application? Is not the connection a very real and vital one between dying and future life? and so the Apostle says that ' he that is *dead* is freed from sin,' *Rom.* v, 27, *i.e.*, is alive to GOD. Cannot it be that this death threatened against the ungodly is, after all, the way, however sharp, to life even for them? Do you remember the words of St. PAUL, *Rom.* xi, 15, ' What shall the reconciling of them be ' but *life from the dead* ; ' on the view generally held these words, so significant to the thoughtful, lose all real force.

And yet you who uphold the popular creed assume that to die is the end of all hope to the sinful. Again, let me ask, on what authority do you teach this doctrine, unknown to antiquity, unknown to Scripture? Who commissioned you to teach, that to die is to pass into a state beyond the reach of CHRIST's grace? If so, why are we told so significantly the story of CHRIST evangelising the spirits in prison? Why does the Apostle tell us that the *Gospel was preached to the dead?* or why these repeated and exultant questions, ' O death where is thy victory ? ' ' O

---

* I confine myself, in attempting to bring out the true significance of 'death,' to the New Testament. In the Old Testament its threatenings, of 'death' and 'destruction,' are, if not exclusively, mainly temporal, as are its rewards.

'death where is thy sting?' Why has the New Testament, with such varied illustrations, pressed on us this fact, that CHRIST has overcome death, has destroyed death, if death is to put a stop to HIS power to save? So far from this, St. PAUL in aid of his argument in the famous chapter on the resurrection, invokes the analogy of nature, as shewing that to die is a path to life, a condition of life. 'Thou fool,' says the great Apostle, 'that which thou sowest is not quickened *except* '*it die*.'

Who shall limit this truth in its operation? It certainly does hold good in many cases in the spiritual order—of that we are assured. 'If we 'be *dead* with HIM, we shall live with HIM.'— *II Tim.* ii, 11. 'We which live are always 'delivered unto *death* for JESUS' sake, that the '*life* also of JESUS might be manifested in us.'— *II Cor.* iv, 11. May not death then be the very instrument by which GOD quickens the sinner, and that in two ways?

i. By the death of the body, which takes a man out of the present age into a state more fitted to rouse and to save.

ii. By the death of the spirit, *i.e.*, its being searched through and through by GOD's fiery discipline—by HIS sharp surgery—till it die to sin and live to righteousness.

In all this subject of death there is a strange

narrowness in the views yet held generally, so unlike the old faith of the Catholic Church—so blindly traditional—as though the fact of dying could change God's unchanging purpose, as though His never failing love were extinguished because we pass into a new state of existence, as though the power of Christ's cross were exhausted in the brief span of our earthly life. So far from this, has not Christ abolished *death*? Is He not Lord of the *dead*? Did He not evangelise the *dead*? Has He not the keys of *death*? On the popular view, what depth of meaning can you assign to these words?

May I be permitted a few words before passing on? What welcome light is thrown by the view of death, just given, on that which else so sorely tries our faith. I mean those very frequent catastrophes which involve in a common destruction the innocent and the guilty—the earthquake —the storm—the pestilence—the famine—the shipwreck—the fire—know no mercy apparently; spare no sex; respect no age. And very often, not merely do the innocent suffer with the guilty, but for the guilty. All this does try—often sorely—and perplex our faith. But how, if *death be a gain*, does not all the strain and perplexity vanish, if we see in death God's angel of mercy, and connect with it thoughts of hope, even for the sinner. Not that I mean for a moment to deny its terrors to the ungodly; but to believe that is quite consistent with a firm faith, that its ultimate purpose is, even for the worst, one of mercy, that, at any rate, to pass through 'the 'gate of death' into a new state of existence is not, and cannot be, to pass beyond the power of CHRIST to save. Although to die may be, nay must be, for the sinner to pass into a state of suffering prolonged, so long as his sin endures, yet even sinners are in CHRIST's hand; and although dead to us, are yet within the reach of the working of that grace which must one day overcome all sin, and sum up all things in HIM who is All and in All.

And what is true of 'death' as threatened against the sinner is true no less of 'judgement,' even in its most extreme form. We are not without very distinct teaching in Holy Scripture on this point. It has been already noticed how, in the minor Prophets, the vision of universal bliss is ever associated with a vision of '*judgement*' (see pp. 93-4). Why is this so significantly done? It is because the way to blessedness lies *through* the divine judgements. In these often unperceived connections lies surely much of the deepest teaching of Holy Scripture. On the popular view this connection of judgement and blessedness loses all meaning.

'Judgement,' in fact, like 'fire,' is the portion of *all*, and not of the sinner merely. It must begin at the House of GOD. 'HE scourgeth *every* son whom HE receiveth.' True—you may say—but what of the sinner, is there hope for him in GOD's judgements? Does GOD's judgement mean mercy in his case? Surely, I reply, of this truth Scripture is full. Take for instance St. PETER's words, as he tells the story of the preaching of CHRIST to the spirits in prison (a passage that even if it stood alone would shew how untenable is the popular view as to the state after death). The spirits are specially described as those of the *disobedient* dead—those who rejected NOAH's preaching. From their case St. PETER turns to speak to the ungodly of his own day, and warns them that they shall have to give account to HIM who is ready to judge the quick and dead. And mark what follows: 'For 'this cause,' he adds, 'was the gospel preached, '(even) to the *dead*, that they might be *judged* 'according to men in the flesh, but *live* according 'to GOD in the spirit.' Is not judgement here most closely related, not to damnation, for the sinner, but to spiritual life, is it not the path to life?

Would you have further proof? Consider next what St. PAUL says of the case of HYMENÆUS and ALEXANDER, *I Tim.* i, 20. They had put away a good conscience, had become blasphemers, had made shipwreck of faith. He thereupon hands *them over to Satan*. You can hardly imagine a more desperate state. Thrust by Apostolic authority out of GOD's Church, and handed over to GOD's enemy, and that after having made shipwreck of their faith. But what follows? it is that they may *learn* not to blaspheme. This terrible judgement was a cure—a path to life and restoration.

In this connection, as shewing how the utmost conceivable severity of the Divine judgements is consistent with final salvation. I ask you next to remember how St. PAUL tells of Israel that 'wrath is come upon them to the uttermost.' —*I Thes.* ii, 16. The wrath of GOD to the *uttermost*! and yet the same Apostle tells us that *all Israel shall be saved!* Suppose it had pleased GOD to withold this later revelation of HIS purpose from our knowledge at present, who would not have said, hope is quite gone? But in fact wrath to the utmost ends in mercy to all.

Another equally striking instance of the connection of judgement with life and amendment, is furnished by St. PAUL's treatment of the incestuous Corinthian. 'I have *judged* already in the 'name of our LORD JESUS CHRIST, to deliver 'such an one *unto Satan* for the destruction of 'the flesh, that the spirit may be *saved* in the 'day of the LORD JESUS.'—*I Cor.* v, 3. Few more suggestive passages exist in the New Testament. Here is a man delivered by Apostolic authority—in the name of JESUS CHRIST—to Satan, handed over to Satan. But mark the object and the result. It is to end not in misery but in joy—not in death but in life—say rather in life attained by means of GOD's awful judgement.* What light is thus thrown (for are not these things written for our learning?) on the mysterious subject of GOD's judgements—nay of HIS vengeance.† " O mon ame sois tranquille " et attends en paix le jour des vengeances eter- " nelles, c'est le jour de CHRIST, et ce sont les " vengeances de CHRIST. C'est donc *un jour de* " *salut et ce sont des vengeances d'amour.*"—G. MONOD, *Le Judgement Dernier*, p. 28. Nay, what light is there not thus reflected on the essential idea and purpose of all the Divine punishments, both here and hereafter: for the unchanging GOD cannot vary HIS great purpose, HIS essential plan, cannot now punish to amend and hereafter change HIS method: to do so HE should change HIS own nature.

Thus you see what the Bible teaches about the divine 'judgements,' even in their very sharpest form. They are remedial and medicinal: they do not, at the very extremest, exclude hope; they are rather the channel through which healing comes. Do you need proofs? Permit me to

---

* " Destruction itself may be the very condition of salvation. " * * * This wretched Corinthian was, as we know, delivered "*from* the power of the Devil by being delivered *into* the power of "the Devil."—*The Larger Hope.*

† Bearing in mind these considerations, can we not understand the otherwise strange insertion of the clause about vengeance in the well known passage describing CHRIST's mission, " To proclaim the " acceptable year of the LORD, and *the day of vengeance* of our GOD." *Isaiah* lxi, 2 ?

repeat briefly, and to emphasise what I have just said. In Holy Scripture we read, as you have just seen, how the wrath of GOD came upon the Jews to *the uttermost*. Weigh well these words and what they convey. It is as though the cup of Divine vengeance was drained to the last drop, as though GOD had exhausted all his vials of anger, and left HIMSELF no more that HE could do. And even then, does all this wrath mean that hope is at an end, that salvation is impossible? It means the very reverse. Not only is hope still remaining, not merely is there a chance of salvation, but salvation is promised, is assured; nay, salvation in its amplest form—salvation to the uttermost (for *all* Israel shall be saved)—is the end of wrath to the uttermost.

Nor is this an isolated example. You have been pointed to the case of HYMENÆUS and ALEXANDER, who—bankrupt in faith, castaway—are handed over to Satan. Can you imagine to all appearance a doom more terrible? and yet it is all done that they may learn not to blaspheme. The judgement has worked a cure, sharp as it has been, it is all but a medicine to *heal* the soul, a process of cure and not of perdition So with the incestuous Corinthian. His case is the same, he, too, is turned over to the evil one; lost surely you will say, if ever a case was hopeless it would be this. But he too is restored, welcomed back to the fold. Lastly, recall those whose case is more striking still—more striking, for in the other cases spiritual healing came in the present life—but in the case of the disobedient Antediluvians they went down to the pit unrepentant. GOD's messenger, NOAH, vainly preached to them. A life of special disobedience was crowned by a death of special judgement; even so is their's then a hopeless doom? Is that the meaning of GOD's judgement? So far from this being so the Bible lifts the veil of the unseen world; tells us how the Gospel message reached these sinners after death, in order that they might be judged according to men in the flesh, but live according to GOD in the spirit.

But next a few words must be added as to the true place 'fire' holds in the teaching of the New Testament. It, like judgement, so far from being the sinners portion only, is the portion of *all*. *Everyone*, says our LORD in a solemn passage (usually misunderstood, *St. Mark* ix, 43-50), *everyone* shall be salted with 'fire.' HE significantly reminds us that HE 'came to send *fire* upon the 'earth.—*S. Luke* xxii, 49. And so "the 'fire' shall "try *every* man's work." Our LORD is described as baptizing his disciples with 'fire.' St. PETER bids his converts not wonder at the 'fiery' trial which they must pass. This was the firm belief of the old Fathers, without perhaps any exception (see note p. 74). Let St. AMBROSE speak. Writing on *Ps.* cxviii, "all," he says, "must be proved by "fire, as many as desire to return to Paradise. "For, not idly has it been written, that when

"ADAM and EVE when driven forth from Para-
"dise, GOD placed at the gate thereof a flaming
"sword which turned every way. *All* then must
"pass through these fires, whether it be that
"JOHN the Evangelist whom the Lord so loved,
"or that PETER who received the keys of the
"Kingdom of Heaven."—*Serm.* xx, 12.

So far from seeking to explain away the solemn warnings of the Gospel, the larger hope in fact presses them home. It warns *everyone* that the way to life lies through the 'fires,' that the cross must either be taken up here and now, or else if sin be indulged in, that there awaits the sinner hereafter a far more terrible ordeal, a Divine 'fire' that shall search him through and through. We, then, who teach hope for all men, do not shrink from, but accept *in their fullest meaning*, those mysterious 'fires' of Gehenna of which CHRIST speaks (kindled for purification), as in a special sense the sinner's doom in the coming ages. If, as the Bible plainly teaches, *all* must pass through 'the fires,' then for the sinner doubtless a far sharper fire must be kindled hereafter. But taught by the clearest statements of Scripture (confirmed as they are by all the analogies of nature), we see in these 'fires' not a denial of but a mode of fulfilling the assured promise—"Behold, I *make all things new.*" They in fact are but mistaking the whole significance of fire in its Scriptural usage who regard it as implying merely torment. Alike nature and Scripture teach a far different lesson as to the uses of 'fire.' Its mission is to *bless* and to *purify*. It sustains life and cherishes it. No doubt it has a mission of destruction, but even then its agency is in the end to promote and call forth fresh life and growth.

Had these facts been borne in mind, how much painful controversy would have been spared ; how many sad hearts would have escaped the suffering of needless pangs, if they had but remembered or been taught the *beneficent* action of fire. For again and again recalling this fact, and trying to impress it on the minds of men no apology is needed. Few more necessary offices can be undertaken by those who treat of this subject than to assert the life-giving, the cleansing, the purifying agency of fire, in opposition to that untrue and gloomy view that looks on it as an agent of mere torment. " Fire,' in Scripture, is " the element of ' life ' (*Is*. iv, 5), of ' purifica- " tion ' (*Matt*. iii, 3), of ' atonement ' (*Lev*. xvi, " 27), of ' transformation ' (*II Peter*, iii, 10), and " at the worst only of ' total destruction ' (*Rev*. " xx, 9), *never of* ' preservation alive' for pur- " poses of anguish." And the popular view selects precisely this latter use, never found in Scripture, and represents it as the *sole* end of GOD's fiery judgements! Need I say more? By such means as this has the traditional creed been built up ; on arguments so unsound, so partial does it rest : arguments whose weakness is brought into clear relief by the very Scriptures to which it appeals, even without considering the abundant evidence furnished by nature of the *beneficent* agency of fire.

There remains for our consideration, a very important class of passages, supposed, but, as I shall hope to shew, erroneously, to favour the popular creed. These passages—to which I would now briefly advert—are those that speak of the 'elect,' and their fewness (see p. 7), of the 'many' called but the 'few' chosen. That GOD's election is a doctrine clearly revealed in Scripture, none can doubt: although, unfortunately, around few subjects has the battle of controversy been so furiously waged. One great party has, in affirming GOD's election—which is true—so affirmed it as to make HIM into an arbitrary and cruel tyrant—which is false. But the truer and deeper views of GOD's plan of mercy through JESUS CHRIST—now in the ascendant, I trust—teach us to affirm distinctly the doctrine of the Divine election of 'the few,' and just because we so affirm it to connect with it purposes of *universal* mercy.

For what is the true end and meaning of GOD's election when rightly understood? The elect, we reply, are chosen, not for themselves only but for others sake. They are 'elect,' not merely to be blessed but to be a source of blessing. GOD's choice of 'the few' is not designed to terminate with them. It is not merely with the paltry object of saving a few, while the vast majority perish, that GOD elects; it is with a Divine purpose, a purpose of mercy to all; it is by 'the few' to save 'the many,' by the elect to save the world. "If you go to Scripture," says Dr. COX, "you will find this its constant "teaching. Even in those early days when one "man, one family, one nation, were successively "chosen, to be the depositories of Divine truth, "when, therefore, if ever we might expect to find "the redemptive purpose of GOD disclosed within "narrow and local limitations, when unquestion- "ably it was much fettered and restrained by "personal promises, and by national and tem- "porary institutions, the Divine purpose is for "ever oversteping every limit, every transient "localisation and restraint, and claiming, as its "proper sphere, all the souls that are and shall "be."

This admits of easy proof. Take a typical case to shew what GOD's election really means. Take the case of ABRAHAM, the father and founder of GOD's elect people. What was the promise to him? 'That in his seed should *all the families of the earth* be blessed.' This was of the essence of GOD's election. And to this effect St. PAUL speaks with perfect clearness. The promise to ABRAHAM was, he tells us, that he should be the heir of the *world, Rom.* iv, 13, words most expressive, and yet without meaning on the common view of election. In other words the Jews, as GOD's people, have, as their inheritance, all lands, all peoples. In the same Epistle (to the Romans) St. PAUL points out how close the connection is between Israel and the world—p.p. 121, 123. Three times over he asserts their very fall to be the riches of the world, and asks if so, what will not the reconciling of Israel be (to the world). In short, on GOD's elect people hangs the lot and destiny of mankind—see *Gal.* iii, 8, and *Acts* iii, 21-5; the latter passage is very interesting. St. PETER there asserts the connection between a *universal* restoration and the promise to ABRAHAM, *i.e.*, his election. These topics have been already touched on in earlier chapters, but without again referring to them here, I could not have given any clear view of the Divine election—as a fact undoubtedly taught in Scripture and yet implying a purpose of mercy to all.

A further admirable illustration of this may be given (furnished by Holy Scripture), from its teaching as to the 'first fruits,' and as to the 'first 'born.' Israel, as GOD's elect, is the 'first fruits' —Israel the 'first born.' But the 'first fruits' imply and pledge the *whole* harvest; the 'first 'born' involve and include in the Divine economy the *whole* family (as indeed has been said in a former chapter). "The first born and first fruits "are the 'few' and the 'little flock,' but these, "although 'first delivered from the curse,' have "*a relation to the whole creation*, which shall be "saved in the appointed times by the first born "seed, that is by CHRIST and HIS body." You thus see that we, so far from denying or weakening the election of the *few*, lay stress on it. Rightly viewed, GOD's electing grace stands, not opposed to but in complete agreement with the widest hope for all men. It becomes indeed a corner stone, so to speak, in the edifice of the world's salvation, for HIS 'elect' few are the very means by which our Father designs to bless all HIS children ; designs to work out HIS plan of universal salvation.

Thus I have tried to shew briefly, and doubtless very imperfectly, what the true teaching of Holy Scripture is as to the 'ages,' 'death,' 'judgement,' 'fire,' and 'election.' It would be easy to add to, and easy to follow out the lines of thought already indicated. Thus, I might shew at length how numerous are the references to 'the ages,' made by the New Testament, how completely this doctrine leavens its pages. As to 'death' it might be pointed out how CHRIST compares it to sleep—but sleep is Nature's restorer. It but refreshes, renews, and invigorates. Again it might be shewn how strikingly the actual state of the world confirms the view given above of 'death.' For it can hardly be doubted that the redemption of CHRIST is meant to be communicated to all those interested in it. But of those born into the world how few, comparatively, have even heard the name of CHRIST in their present state of being. In fact, with singular infelicity, does the popular creed at once unduly exalt and unduly depress our present life; unduly exalt it by representing it as the sole period in which CHRIST's grace can effectually reach the sinner; unduly depress it, by adjourning to a distant future its most solemn facts, forgetting that already 'the solemnities of eternity enfold us,' that already we are standing at the tribunal * of GOD, that HIS 'judgements' are now and ever in session, HIS 'fires' are already kindled. How, then, shall these change their essential nature? how shall HIS 'judgements' cease to be remedial? HIS 'fires' cease to be beneficent and purifying? merely because we experience the change called death?

---

* So in *St. Matt.* xiii, 39-40-49, all the solemn imagery of these parables does not belong to the final close of the world, but of 'the age'—see margin of Rev. Ver. The same may very probably be said of the great judgement scene in *St. Matt.* xxv—see p. 152.

"SUMMARY AND CONCLUSION."

"Ye have seen the *end* of the LORD : that the LORD is very pitiful and of tender mercy."—*St. James* v, 11.

"But it shall come to pass that *at evening time it shall be light.*"—Zech. xiv, 7.

"Be the day weary or be it long,
"Still it ringeth to evensong." SKELTON.

"The little Pilgrim listened with an intent face, clasping her hands and said, 'But it never could be that our Father should be overcome by evil. Is that not known in all the worlds?'"—*The Little Pilgrim*, p. 122.

"This world is strange and often terrible; but be not afraid, all will come right at last. Rest will conquer Restlessness; Faith will conquer Fear; Order will conquer Disorder; Health will conquer Sickness; Joy will conquer Sorrow; Pleasure will conquer Pain; Life will conquer Death; Right will conquer Wrong. *All will be well at last.*"—*Madam How and Lady Why*—C. KINGSLEY.

"CHRISTO dedit Pater omne judicium. Poterit ergo te ille damnare, quem redemit a morte, pro quo se obtulit, cujus istam suæ mortis mercem esse cognoscit? Nonne dicet, *quæ utilitas in sanguine meo si damno quem ipse salvavi?*"—S. AMBROSE—*De Jacob. et Vit. Beat.*

CHAPTER X.

SUMMARY AND CONCLUSION.

It is now time to draw to a close these pages, briefly to sum up the course of the argument, and to state the conclusions at which we have arrived. I have shewn, first, how completely impossible it is to reconcile the belief in endless torment with the plain and unmistakeable convictions of our moral nature, God's highest gift to us. Few things are more wonderful in this whole question than the reluctance so many feel to follow out these unhesitating convictions to their *only possible* legitimate conclusion, the rejection of that dogma which so flatly contradicts them. It is not intended for a moment to assert that these convictions are an absolutely infallible guide; for indeed of what can it be said that its directions reach us in an infallible form? Can that be said of the Bible itself? Are those who translate it infallible? Are those who comment on it infallible? Are those who read it free from error, from prejudice, from ignorance? But no one therefore doubts its divine authority, or fails to see in it a guide practically sufficient, and binding on us. Exactly so in the case of that other and primary revelation of GOD to the heart and conscience of man. Although we do not claim infallibility for all its conclusions, yet we do claim that the deliberate verdict of our moral sense represents to us the voice of GOD practically. And therefore that which contradicts our deepest moral intuitions, convictions, instincts (call them what you please), *cannot be true*. Nay, by these very convictions, and by these alone, it is, that life is ordered, that society subsists, that religion itself becomes possible. Now this being so, we cannot dare, as the popular creed does, to attribute to our Creator acts, which we know and feel would be utterly cruel and horrible in an earthly parent. It is a blasphemy against our Maker so to do, it is doubly a blasphemy against HIM who is "our Father." Again, of the untold evil caused by teaching endless torture in Hell as part of the *good* news which JESUS CHRIST came to bring, I have spoken, and have pointed out that it has done more to produce unbelief than probably all other causes put together.

An important point has been briefly discussed (p. 21-2), viz: the attempt made to remove the overwhelming moral difficulties attending the popular creed, by asserting that endless torments are but the result of the human will freely choosing evil; so that, as the phrase is sometimes put, the doors of Hell are " locked on the "inside." Now if this phrase be designed to convey that myriads upon myriads of creatures, children of a GOD, absolute in goodness and in power, will continue deliberately to choose evil to all eternity, I can only repeat that the real difficulties are *not so much as touched* * by any such theory. The intellectual difficulty remains the same, for the Almighty is thus defeated; the Scriptural difficulty remains the same, for its promises of universal restitution come to naught; and the moral difficulty is untouched, for the final victory remains with the powers of darkness on this view.

But I have no space here to attempt any complete summary of the difficulties (already indicated in chs. ii-iii), moral, intellectual, and practical, that beset the popular view. One instance only I can give. All our creeds describe GOD as Almighty: but if this be *true* then it follows that the purposes of such a Being cannot fail, nor His will be resisted with success. And yet the ordinary creed presents to us *Omnipotence*

---

* And the same may be said of the various modifications of the popular creed now current—such as, that not bodily but mental pain will be the penalty inflicted on 'the lost'—or that a sort of maimed and crippled existence, not wholly or not very painful, will be their doom—or that 'the lost' will, after some torments, be annihilated—of all these varying theories not one touches the real difficulties as stated above.

practically *impotent*; a design to save all men (for this cannot be denied if the Bible speaks truly), formed by the Almighty, and formed only to fail. What a weapon to place in the hands of the sceptic! "You have, in fact," he will say, "two "unequal measures,[*] two varying standards of "truth. Which am I to accept? Am I, or am "I not, to believe in the Almighty Being your "creeds proclaim—am I to accept your theory, "or your practical belief? Am I to confess my "faith in the irresistible and unchanging will of "GOD, or shall I believe that this *irresistible* will "may be so successfully resisted as to plunge "half creation into chaos and ruin?"

From these weighty matters we passed on to consider the authorised teaching of the Church. I have shewn you how, in spite of the doctrine of *reserve*, then widely prevalent, and specially applicable to such a dogma as the larger hope, not a few of the greatest of the early Fathers taught, more or less openly, the salvation of all mankind. Further, we have seen how the attempt to procure a condemnation of this belief in the case of ORIGEN signally failed, and how in fact no general council has ever condemned it,

---

[*] You can in fact justify the popular creed in one way, and in that alone, by attaching to each term we apply to GOD two contradictory meanings. HE is Almighty and yet not Almighty, good and yet not good, in the only sense we connect with the word; loving and yet not loving, a Father and yet not a Father, etc.

thus leaving it, so far as the Church is concerned, a perfectly open question. Nor have we omitted to remark how the two Ancient Creeds—the Apostles' and the Nicene—close their statements of Christian truth by the assertion of a belief in *the life to come*, and are *significantly silent* as to anything more than this. In our Book of Common Prayer again, fashioned as it is on the old lines, not a few passages have been noticed that imply the larger hope, and teach, more or less, directly the salvation of all men.

From the Church we turned to consider the all important question of the teaching of Holy Scripture. I have pointed out how, even in the Old Testament, there are intimations from the very first of a future blessing, designed to embrace all the race of man. These intimations become more and more distinct as the plan of GOD is more fully disclosed, and both Psalmists and Prophets unite in their promises of a golden age yet to come, when the knowledge of the LORD shall cover the earth as the waters cover the sea. The New Testament received more minute attention, due to its supreme importance. The passages—at least the most important ones—supposed generally to teach the popular creed, have been carefully considered, and we have seen reason to conclude that they, one and all, while emphatically warning sinners of wrath to come, teach nowhere an *endless* punishment, nowhere an unending Hell.

Next, I have dwelt on this surely very suggestive fact, that in not a few cases the very arguments from Scripture, alleged in favour of the popular creed, do in fact, when fairly understood, teach the reverse. Thus you remember how a chapter was devoted to a brief discussion of certain classes of texts, usually quoted in favour of the popular belief, *e.g.*, those speaking of GOD's 'election of the few,' of 'death,' of 'judgement,' of 'fire,' of 'the ages.' I have attempted to shew that the true teaching of Holy Scripture on all these points is in absolute harmony with the larger hope; that to insist on one and all of these points is but to bring into clearer relief the doctrine of universal salvation.

And as the larger hope leads us to affirm and emphasise the teaching of Scripture as to the guilt of actual sin and its certain punishment, so it teaches us to give prominence to the fact of original sin. For in this it sees a clear proof of a fundamental doctrine of Scripture, the organic unity of our race; a doctrine lying at the root of the Fall and the Incarnation. Each infant born into a state of sin is a witness to its truth, and bears in its whole life sad proof of the organic unity of our race in the taint drawn from our first parent ADAM. But this unity is to be traced not alone in the tie connecting us with the first ADAM, but as truly in the bond which unites us with the second ADAM. In words admitted—this is in fact denied by the popular creed—but once admitted as a vital fact, it follows necessarily that CHRIST's relation is not to men singly, but to man, *i.e.*, mankind. Therefore the salvation which HE brings is not (cannot be) a thing of individuals, but of all. Therefore a partial salvation is not possible, for CHRIST redeems, not individual men, but mankind ; not human beings severally, but humanity. CHRIST has nothing to do with a part of our race. As the second ADAM HE sums up in HIMSELF and saves the human race, " For as in ADAM all die, so in (the second) " ADAM shall all be made alive."

I have also pointed out that it is not the larger hope, but the popular creed, that in fact teaches men to think lightly of sin, by teaching, as it does, that GOD means to tolerate its presence for ever in HIS universe. And so with GOD's punishments, how often is it not said that those who maintain the final salvation of all men do not believe in future punishment at all, or at least rob GOD's penalties of all meaning by their belief. Exactly the opposite, I reply, is the fact. For the true end of punishment is only clearly recognized when it is seen that—although no doubt retributive—it is essentially remedial and medicinal. To affirm this as the end of all GOD's penalties is to bring into clear relief and not to ignore the Divine punishments. Further, it must be said, that these punishments gain, both in clearness and in certainty, when they are taught in a reasonable form, for then, and then only, do they elicit a response from the conscience and deter, in fact, from the commission of sin.

But our examination of the New Testament has not been confined to the general points just referred to. Two chapters, vi and vii, have been devoted to a series of notes, designedly brief and simple, pointing out how full the New Testament is of passages (alas, neglected or explained away), and yet distinctly teaching or implying the final salvation of all men. So deeply important is this evidence furnished by the New Testament in favour of a universal salvation, that I venture here to append a brief summary of the passages already quoted.

In chapter vi the evidence furnished by the writings of the Evangelists has been considered. Let me point out how clear it is, how emphatic. Thus we have seen how to CHRIST is assigned a kingdom absolutely without bound or limit;* how *all* flesh are to see the salvation HE gives. You have read how the leaven of His Kingdom must work on till the *whole* is leavened, and the Good Shepherd seek on till each sheep HE has lost is found. You have read how the Son of Man came to seek and save, not some of the lost, but simply " that which was lost," *i.e.*, simply " the " lost." HIS mission is again described as having

---

* The passages alluded to, in these and the following paragraphs, have been already given at length in chs. vi-vii.

as its object the salvation of the world, and HE is said *to take away* the sin of the whole world. Do these terms fairly represent a partial salvation, are they honestly consistent with it? Again, it is said that *all things* have been given to the Son, and that all that is so given shall come to HIM. HE is repeatedly described as the Saviour of the world (which yet HE does not in fact save on the popular view), as the Light of the world. HE is said not to offer but to *give* life to the world; a totally different thing! HE says (no words can be more absolute), speaking of HIS Cross, that HE will draw *all* men unto HIMSELF. HE adds, that HE came not to judge, but to save the world.

All these passages are familiar: true, but can you possibly on any fair theory of the meaning of human language reconcile them with the horrors of an endless Hell, or with a partial salvation? If the sin of the *whole world be taken away*, how shall there be a Hell for its endless punishment? If *all* things without exception (the original is the widest possible), are given to CHRIST, and all so given to HIM shall come to HIM, can you reconcile this with unending misery? But let us go on: we find language over and over again employed by the Evangelists quite as strong and as decisive against the popular creed, as that just quoted. When, for instance, we read in *St. John* how GOD's Son was manifested for the very purpose of *sweeping away the works of the Devil*;

is that consistent by any possibility with the preserving these works in Hell? Is there no significance in CHRIST's telling us that HE is "alive unto the ages, and has the *keys* of Hell "and death?" Or again, what does the promise to make *all* things new mean? If this be not a promise of universal restoration, what is it? Again, remember the promise that there shall be no more curse, and *no more pain*. Lastly, ponder over the glorious vision of the *Apocalypse*, where every creature in Heaven, on earth, and under the earth, is described as joining in the song of praise to GOD and to the Lamb; and ask yourself if less than a universal salvation can possibly satisfy the plain sense of these words of Scripture. Such are some passages already quoted, see chapter vi; and yet these are by no means the whole of the evidence the New Testament furnishes, we have next to consider a very large body of fresh passages quite as strong, quite as distinctly teaching the same truth, furnished by the Epistles of St. PAUL, St. PETER, and that to the *Hebrews* (see chapter vii).

St. PAUL's Epistles especially are full of the most glowing anticipations of the universal reign of CHRIST, and the assured triumph of HIS Kingdom over evil and sin. Thus ABRAHAM is to receive the world, and no less, as HIS portion, *i.e.*, in GOD's elect seed all are to be saved. Whatever the Fall has done to injure man is to be repaired, and much more than repaired, by the gift of GOD's grace in CHRIST. But is it possible to undo *all* that sin has done if a single soul be left in endless loss? would not St. PAUL be in fact speaking *untruly* in such a case? Further, the same apostle assures us that the *whole creation* shall be delivered into the glorious liberty of GOD's children. And again he argues that the very fact of GOD's giving His Son proves that with HIM all things are given—the original word is the widest possible, and certainly includes all souls. Again *all* Israel are to be saved (and Israel's salvation is that of the world, see p. 123), for, adds the Apostle, GOD's gifts and calling are undefeasible: words significant in the highest degree, for what is the popular creed but an emphatic assertion that GOD's calling may be defeated, and GOD's gifts set at naught? And what St. PAUL here asserts is echoed in the Epistle to the *Hebrews*, which assures us of the immutability of GOD's counsel. Again has GOD shut up *all* in unbelief, it is, St. PAUL says, that HE may have mercy upon *all*. Does *all* mean 'some' in the latter clause, and not in the former here?

Once more, the same Apostle assures us—and mark these words, for they are surely conclusive—that if the first ADAM brings death universally, then the second ADAM is to bring universal life. If sin abounds, *much more* shall grace abound. Weigh these words well, for in saying that the second ADAM has in fact failed in myriads of cases to undo the evil caused by the Fall, you are giving these words of Scripture the flattest contradiction that it is possible to give. Then as to CHRIST's empire, the Apostle says it must extend universally, that to HIM *every* knee must bow, and *every* tongue confess; that one day—at the end—GOD shall be *all in all*. In fact St. PAUL never seems to weary of claiming this universal dominion for CHRIST. *All* things are to be gathered together in one in CHRIST (not in Hell surely!) words repeated even more emphatically when the Apostle asserts that by the blood of the Cross *all* things have been reconciled unto the Father. Does the reconciliation of all things, *i.e.*, the universe, by the Cross mean the sending of countless myriads to endless pain? Further, the Apostle assures us that the living GOD is the Saviour of *all*, that JESUS CHRIST has *abolished death*, that the grace of GOD bringeth salvation to *all* men. Are these statements consistent with a partial salvation?

St. PETER too, speaks to the same effect. You remember that he tells the wonderful story of CHRIST preaching *to the dead* who had once been disobedient and were apparently *lost*; a story whose significance is the very greatest possible, as indicating how behind the veil CHRIST works on to heal and to save: and in his second Epistle adds, that the Lord is not willing that *any* should perish. Is GOD's deliberate counsel—such is the original word—to come to nothing? Then in

SUMMARY AND CONCLUSION

the Epistle to the *Hebrews* we have some remarkable testimony to the same effect. Thus we have there repeated the assertion that *all* things are to be put under CHRIST ; that HIS object in dying was to destroy the Devil, that once in the end of the age has HE appeared to put away, *i.e* , *abolish sin* by HIS sacrifice of HIMSELF. Do say how the abolition of sin is or can be consistent with the maintaining of evil in Hell for ever ? Finally let me remind you how precise and emphatic the promise is (see *Hebrews* viii, 10-1), that one day *all* shall know the LORD, from the least to the greatest.

Such is a very brief outline of the teaching of Scripture, for I have not by any means cited here all its promises of universal salvation. It is, you see, no case of isolated texts. It is no case of building upon Eastern metaphors, of dogma resting upon misconceptions of the original. It is quite the contrary. It is evidence, clear and unambiguous, and not this alone but repeated over and over again as we have seen. You have, in fact, line upon line, promise upon promise, assertions, *varied, reiterated, accumulated*, yet amid all their variety pointing with one consent to this great central thought, to the *completeness of the triumph of Jesus Christ*, to the boundless nature of HIS empire over all souls ; to the assurance of a victory, infinite and absolute, won by HIS incarnation, HIS death, and HIS resurrection, over all the powers of evil.

This being so, let me next ask, have you who maintain the popular creed, ever quietly thought over the terrible slight you offer to the whole work of CHRIST, to HIS incarnation and HIS passion, by asserting the final loss of countless myriads of our race? He has come, we know, to save the world. HE, the *Almighty* One; *very God of very God*: but you are never tired of proclaiming in all your writings, in all your pulpits, HIS defeat! HIS Apostles announce, in language strong and clear, in words that still burn and throb with life, HIS victory over death. You announce death's victory over HIM, for Hell filled to all eternity with its wailing millions is HIS defeat, nay HIS utter defeat. Could you more effectually make light of HIS atonement? Could you, in fact, more truly pour scorn on HIS Cross and Passion? I read in HIS word, that in HIS death all (actually) died, (so vital, so close is the union between HIM and all the race of man). Are they then to go down to endless pains, those lost ones *who died with Jesus* (see p. 126), those souls of HIS creating, of HIS redeeming, still wet, so to speak, with HIS most precious blood, still pursued by HIS love (for love is unfailing), are these souls to spend an eternity of torment? Am I to proclaim this as the victory of JESUS CHRIST, this as the glad tidings of great joy?

Do allow me further, for I want again and again to protest against the dishonour done to GOD's word by the popular creed—do allow me before I leave this solemn subject, to ask what the meaning is on the popular view, of the oft repeated promises of the New Testament to CHRIST of a universal empire? What do they mean, if they do not really mean, that to CHRIST'S kingdom there shall one day be actually no limit? *Is it true*, in the natural acceptance of the words, that in CHRIST *all things*, *Eph.* i, 10—the original words are the widest possible—are to be summed up. Is it *true* that CHRIST has actually abolished death; that HE has been manifested for this very end, that HE might destroy *all* the works of the Devil? Or is it a mere dream of the Evangelist when he tells us that GOD has given to HIM all things, and that all things that the Father hath given to HIM shall come to HIM? But if all this, and far, far more than this, is actually written in Holy Scripture, do explain how it is that you can teach that sin is eternal, ruin eternal, Hell eternal? What! sin everlasting, and yet the sins of the world taken away by the Lamb of GOD. Hell for ever preying on the countless tribes of the lost, and yet the whole creation delivered into the glorious liberty of the children of GOD.

Do but reflect and see what it is you are, in fact, teaching. CHRIST "holding the keys of "Hell" and never opening! CHRIST "making all "things new," and yet things and persons innumerable not renewed! The Good Shepherd "seeking till HE finds," and yet never finding!

"No more pain," and yet pain for evermore! "No more curse," and yet Hell echoing forever with the curses of the lost! "Tears wiped from "every eye," and yet the lost forever weeping! "Every creature which is in Heaven and on the "earth and under the earth, and such as are on "the sea and all that are in them, saying blessing "and glory and honour to GOD" and yet an infinite number of creatures shut up for ever and ever in misery! "All made alive in CHRIST," and yet myriads sunk in hopeless, endless death.

Finally, what remains to say? It remains only that I plead for the acceptance of the larger hope, as taught and believed by so many in primitive days; a hope, and a firm faith that it has ever been the purpose of our Father to save all HIS human children. To believe less than this would be, not alone to contradict the plain and repeated teachings of Holy Scripture, as I have tried to shew, but to mistake its whole scope and purpose. For what is the Bible? it is the story of a Restoration, wider, deeper, mightier than the Fall, and therefore bringing to every child of ADAM healing and salvation. It is not, as the popular creed teaches, the self-contradictory story of One Almighty to save and yet not, in fact, saving those for whom HE died. It is the story of infinite love seeking "till it find," a love that never faileth, never, though Heaven and earth pass away. It is the story of the unchanging purpose of the unchanging GOD.

SUMMARY AND CONCLUSION. 213

Further, by this larger hope, and by *it alone*, can we accept and harmonize every line and letter of Holy Scripture, its solemn threatenings to the sinner, no less than its repeated promises of life to all. These threatenings I accept implicitly. They are, as we have seen, fully reconciled with the promises of universal salvation the moment we have learned to realise the true meaning of GOD's judgements and penalties, and led by HIS word to see in 'the ages' yet to come HIS purposes being steadily worked out.

Yes, I believe, because the New Testament so teaches and all reason confirms it, that to this brief life there succeed many ages, and that " through these ages an increasing purpose runs." In these 'ages' and during their progress it is that GOD's threatenings find their complete fulfilment for the ungodly, and the many successive scenes of the drama of redemption are slowly unfolded, and carried to completion. For God's purpose to save all men once declared must stand firm for ever from His very nature; and to this end it is that HIS penalties are inflicted, that in JESUS CHRIST one day all created things may be summed up. And this being so, we who hold the larger hope are prepared fully to believe that there await the sinner in ' the ages' yet to come, GOD's fiery judgements; that æonian discipline protracted till the will of man yield to the will of " our Father," and till, as in the silent prophecy of the familiar words, " that will be done on earth "as it is in heaven."

For this I plead, for a hope, wide as that which swelled the Saviour's heart, when looking steadily at the Cross HE said "I, if I be lifted up will "draw all men unto me." I plead for the simple truthfulness of the explicit promise made by all GOD's Holy Prophets, that there shall be a 'resti-'tution of all things," *Acts* iii, 21. The issue may be simply stated, *is this promise true* or *is it untrue?* The dilemma cannot be avoided—*yes* or *no?*

For my part, in this promise I believe—in the true catholicity of the Church of CHRIST, as destined to embrace all mankind, in the power of HIS redemption, as something which no will can resist, to which all things must yield one day in perfect submission, love and harmony. I plead for the acceptance of this great central truth, that the victory of JESUS CHRIST must be final, absolute, and complete—that nothing can impair the power of HIS Cross and Passion to save the human race. I believe that HE shall see of the travail of HIS soul, and be satisfied. And I feel assured that less than a world saved, a universe restored, could not satisfy the heart of JESUS CHRIST, or the love of our Father. Therefore in these pages I have pleaded for the larger hope. Therefore I believe in the vision, glorious beyond all power of human thought fully to realise, of a 'Paradise regained,' of a universe from which every stain of sin shall have been swept away, in which every heart shall be full of blessedness, in which "God shall be all and in all."—*Amen.*

NOTES.

On St. Mark ix, 43-50.

I think a dispassionate reader will see at once that the key to this passage lies in the clause which assigns the reason of the whole preceding verses. 'For *every one* must 'be salted with fire.' In fact, JESUS CHRIST is here warning HIS disciples—not that sinners will go to Hell, but that there is no possibility for any one to escape the 'fire.' HE states this in terms highly figurative, which allude to the Jewish law of sacrifice—which enjoined salt in every meat offering—'All must be salted with fire.' In other words, sacrifice is the great Christian law. If the eye which offends be not voluntarily plucked out, then a sharper sacrifice will be exacted—a more intense salting with fire will be required, *i.e.*, with the fire of Gehenna. To revert to the law of sacrifice—which explains this—we must remember that the sin offering was cast out without the camp, and there burned. This answers to Gehenna in the text, which lay outside the city. Such a fiery sacrifice will be exacted, says our Lord, from those who neglect to sacrifice themselves.

But it is said, this fire 'is not quenched' and 'the worm 'dieth not.' Assuredly; but this very phrase, 'the fire is 'not quenched' is but a quotation from the Old Testament, where it *has no such meaning* as the popular view asserts— nor any meaning at all similar. It occurs applied first to the burnt offering in *Lev.* vi, 13. The words of the Septuagint there, are the very same as those of the text here. They imply no thought of endless burning—still less of endless suffering—but are, in fact, an equivalent to such a phrase as this, 'there is a fire always burning.' They are used just as if we were to say, 'on the altar the fire is con- 'stantly burning;' but that would imply no assertion that the fire would go on literally for ever and ever. Any such assertion would be a distinct perversion of Scripture there, and assuredly is so here.

ON THE FUTURE RECOVERY OF THE LOST.

In speaking of punishment as remedial as well as retributive, we do not mean that it alone can effect any change in the nature of those undergoing the sentence. The great medicinal agencies of the future are assumed to be the same as those now bringing salvation to the lost and guilty, viz., The love of God through Jesus Christ, by the operation of the Holy Spirit, can alone complete the recovery of the human race. By what particular channels these are to be applied we do not presume to state with any exactness where Scripture is silent. But an enquirer may be reminded that many of the existing agencies may well be conceived to work on in the future ages, and to work then under conditions more favourable than those now in force, in a new and wholly spiritual state, when our eyes, now holden, shall have been fully opened.

Nothing forbids our believing that the Church's mission to the lost may be continued in the coming ages, nor that fresh agencies may be added—fresh ministries of love and of fear—ministries on the part of higher intelligences, with whom, when the veil is lifted, we may be permitted to hold direct personal communion. Nay, who shall prevent our hoping and believing that Jesus Christ himself, who is "*the same unto the ages,*" will still behind the veil, seek on and on till the last wanderer be found.

CPSIA information can be obtained
at www.ICGtesting.com
Printed in the USA
LVOW04s2301170516
488766LV00031B/384/P

9 781104 399221